"Jordan Ballor has written a useful guide for those wishing to venture into the smelly swamps of ecumenical social and economic thought. Why should non-swamp dwellers care what goes on there? Ballor's quite reasonable answer is that ecumenical bodies claim to speak on behalf of churches, churches which many of us are part. Whether anyone outside is listening is another question—one which Ballor doesn't address but which others such as Anthony Waterman have considered—that being less and less so. Ballor's book is distinguished by considering not just the content of ecumenical statements on economic matters (which have given grief to a long line of professional economists), but also the theological self-understanding of the various bodies when they speak. He asks the deeper question of whether the bodies are adequately constituted to be the (or even a) Christian voice on economic matters, as well as the not irrelevant questions of their actual theological and economic competence. Fundamental questions are raised about the relationship between theological and economic discourse, and the sorts of institutions that support helpful discourse. Christian faith certainly bears on economic matters—the briefest acquaintance with the Scriptures is enough to dispel any doubts. Ballor's book is part of the movement towards a better discussion of the links in our churches, universities and political forums."

PAUL OSLINGTON
Professor of Economics,
Australian Catholic University, and Visiting Fellow,
St. Mark's National Theological Centre
and Australian Centre for Christianity and Culture, Canberra

"With *Ecumenical Babel* Jordan J. Ballor gives us a much needed consideration of modern ecumenism. In particular he grapples with this daunting question: whether ecumenical bodies indeed speak for the church in their pronouncements on the hot-button social issues of the day. Wedding compassion with clear-headed thinking, Ballor questions whether ecumenical bodies may rightfully make such assertions on behalf of God's people, and—more to the point—whether ecumenism is getting its economics right."

VICTOR V. CLAAR
Associate Professor of Economics,
Henderson State University,
and coauthor, *Economics in Christian Perspective:
Theory, Policy and Life Choices*

"Drawing on a long running and coherent critique that begins with Dietrich Bonhoeffer and is picked up later by Paul Ramsey, *Ecumenical Babel* explains why the activism of the social justice curia of churches and ecumenical bodies so often works at cross purposes to the great moral imperatives of the Judeo-Christian tradition. This is particularly so in the areas that are receiving so much attention now—social ethics and economic globalization. Jordan Ballor vividly illustrates how the ideologies of these church bureaucracies are grounded in faulty economic thinking, which leads to policy positions that seem to be impervious to the facts of the situation. *Ecumenical Babel* is an invaluable introduction to the world of contemporary ecumenical social thought and should be required reading for anyone interested in the future of Christian social witness."

MICHAEL CROMARTIE
Vice President, Ethics and Public Policy Center,
and Vice Chair, United States Commission
on International Religious Freedom

"Inter-Christian dialogue is more important than ever as Christendom lurches from one crisis to the next. The problem is that many of the bodies created to foster this dialogue end up beholden to neo-Marxist, collectivist, and statist paradigms that ostensibly solve the crisis but are in fact no more than temporalized, millennial knock-offs of the Christian faith. Jordan Ballor offers us a short history of strong Protestant thinkers (Dietrich Bonhoeffer, Paul Ramsey, and Ernest Lefever) who recognized the vulnerability of these ecumenical bodies to the ideologically inclined. In *Ecumenical Babel*, the author reminds us that the original intention of ecumenical dialogue was not to subvert the Christian social witness, but discern how to bring it into an increasingly secular world—a world that every day seems to drift farther from its moral moorings. The takeover of the WCC, NCC, and other groups by ideologues represents neither a corruption of the original intent of the ecumenical movement, nor does it represent the inevitable end of the dialogue. Rather, the lesson of failure is that we learn, once more, what Bonhoeffer and Ramsey and Lefever taught: We follow no one but Christ."

REV. JOHANNES L. JACOBSE
President, American Orthodox Institute

"Jordan Ballor calls for leaders of the largest Christian ecumenical organizations to stop endorsing neo-Marxist hermeneutics as the presumed framework for Christian professions of social theory and practice worldwide. He appeals to Dietrich Bonhoeffer and Paul Ramsey in making a case for welcoming diversity of theological and economic opinion on Christianity and the emerging modern global economic culture, and for encouraging debate as the best means for making confessions on Christian social policy. Ballor draws upon the recent works of Christian writers who resist neo-Marxist deconstructions of market capitalism as *inherently* de-humanizing and destructive to the natural world. On the contrary, they see immense potential in market capitalism for the pursuit of Christian good, not least for the sake of the poor. Ballor's voice is one that very much needs to be heard and considered by all Christians who profess serious commitment to the liberation of the world's poor from the terrible evils of poverty."

JOHN R. SCHNEIDER
Professor of Theology, Calvin College,
and author, *The Good of Affluence:
Seeking God in a Culture of Wealth*

"The modern ecumenical movement, which began a century ago with such promise for unity in the mission of Christ, took a tragic turn at mid-century. As a result of this turn various organizations representing the movement embraced an agenda that is less known for fidelity to the gospel of grace than it is for a sectarian form of culture-Christianity deeply rooted in economic and social theories that are highly questionable. Through a judicious use of source material, and the insights of three great mainstream Christian thinkers from the twentieth century, Jordan Ballor shows why we should end the tyranny of these ecumenical experts and again confess the gospel properly, which is nothing less than the original purpose of ecumenism."

JOHN H. ARMSTRONG
President, ACT 3, and author,
*Your Church Is Too Small:
Why Unity in Christ's Mission
Is Vital to the Future of the Church*

"The economic questions of our age remain widely disputed. Ballor's latest work achieves two objectives: establishing a normative evangelical statement on economics informed by theological thinking, while setting a general basis from which one can posit an informed foundation for any treatment of poverty and economics. Ballor calls into question the basis for some of the past and current premises used to analyze social concerns. Through a reading of the philosophical assumptions that have informed much of the ecumenical analysis on economic issues, Ballor moves to offer an alternative, yet historically consistent Evangelical Protestant framework, from which to address critical social concerns. Ballor meticulously sets out the nature of the demands of moral duty as it relates to the task of soundly formulating prudential judgments. He does so by drawing an important distinction between absolute ends and the misguided effort to standardize proposed economic means as absolute moral positions to which the Christian is bound. Though not an Evangelical Protestant myself, I have found Ballor's work to be of foundational importance: certainly required reading for students, clergy and academics seeking an introductory understanding on how to approach biblical stewardship. The monograph is an excellent starting point to any effort seeking to gather a unified body of Evangelical Protestant thought on the subject."

GARRETH BLOOR
Journalist and Graduate Student
(Social Science Hons.),
University of Cape Town, South Africa

ECUMENICAL
BABEL
CONFUSING ECONOMIC IDEOLOGY
AND THE CHURCH'S SOCIAL WITNESS

ECUMENICAL
BABEL

CONFUSING ECONOMIC IDEOLOGY
AND THE CHURCH'S SOCIAL WITNESS

Jordan J. Ballor

Foreword by Stephen J. Grabill

GRAND RAPIDS · MICHIGAN

Ecumenical Babel: Confusing Economic Ideology and the Church's Social Witness

©2010 by Jordan J. Ballor

Cover image: Marten Van Valckenborch I (1534–1612), Tower of Babel
Source: Art Renewal Center

ISBN 10 : 1-880595-70-2
ISBN 13 : 978-1-880595-70-1

British Library Cataloguing in Publication Information Available

Library of Congress Cataloging-in-Publication Data

Ballor, Jordan J.
      Ecumenical Babel: Confusing Economic Ideology
      and the Church's Social Witness / Ballor, Jordan J.

CHRISTIAN'S LIBRARY PRESS
   *An imprint of the Acton Institute
   for the Study of Religion & Liberty*

161 Ottawa Avenue, NW, Suite 301
Grand Rapids, Michigan 49503
Phone: 616.454.3080
Fax: 616.454.9454
www.clpress.com

*Cover design by Peter Ho
Interior composition by Judy Schafer*

Printed in the United States of America

In necessariis unitas,
in non necessariis libertas,
in omnibus prudentia et caritas.

CONTENTS

FOREWORD

In the preface, Jordan Ballor astutely observes that the year 2010 marks a number of milestones in the life of the contemporary ecumenical movement with the assemblies of the mainline Lutheran World Federation and the newly formed World Communion of Reformed Churches. These are significant events in and of themselves, but 2010 will also mark a milestone for global evangelical ecumenical activity with the convening of the Third Lausanne Congress on World Evangelization in Cape Town, South Africa, October 16–25. Cape Town 2010, held in collaboration with the World Evangelical Alliance, will bring together four thousand leaders from more than two hundred countries to confront the critical issues of our time—other world faiths, poverty, HIV/AIDS, persecution, and mobilizing God's resources to unleash generosity in his people among others as they relate to the future of the church and world evangelization. Thousands more leaders will participate in the discussion on the issues through the Lausanne Global Conversation and at remote Congress sites through the Cape Town GlobaLink. Both mainline Protestants and evangelicals will be simultaneously wrestling with questions concerning the relationship among theology, ethics, economics, and how to most effectively develop models of sustainable ministry to further God's kingdom in the globalized twenty-first century.

Clearly, these questions raise critical discussion points pertaining to method and principle, around which well-meaning Christians can and surely will disagree. It is in light of this recognition that I wish to affirm my colleague's acknowledgment that the purpose of his primer "is certainly not to be the last word on the matter or to confirm those who have abandoned ecumenical work at various levels and with various institutions in their choice." Therefore, neither social quietism, which holds that the church has no public responsibility beyond a bare proclamation of the gospel nor social gospel, which identifies social action on behalf of the poor, the marginalized, and the abused with the gospel itself, are acceptable alternatives.

The recent promulgation of the social encyclical *Caritas in Veritate* (Charity in Truth) by Pope Benedict XVI brings to the fore a host of critical issues confronting all Christians and people of good will in the struggle to address the economy, the defense of life, the promotion of truth, and the witness of love in the pursuit of integral human development. For sympathetic Protestant and evangelical observers of Catholic social doctrine, it also raises the issue of the ongoing need for theological definition and cultural engagement by Protestant and evangelical writers of the concerns that the pope touches on in *Caritas in Veritate*. There is a problem, however, and it is systemic in nature. Neither mainline Protestants nor evangelicals have a theologically unified body of social teaching.

As you may already be aware, Protestant social thought is a vibrant field that, on the one hand, is ever expanding and alert to emerging issues, but it is also, on the other hand, a field that lacks fundamental definition, systematic rigor, and coherence among its various branches. The distinguished Protestant ethicist James Gustafson once described the state of Protestant social thought as "only a little short of chaos," as Ballor notes in his study. Roman Catholic commentators have also pointed out that Protestant social thought operates without an ecclesial magisterium wherein disparate ideas, goals, definitions, and theological affirmations are honed into a body of authoritative social teaching. The question of *how* to build such a body of Protestant social doctrine is one concern, but the issue of *whether* it is even possible to do so within the decentralized strictures of Protestant theology is another entirely.

In recent decades, Protestant and evangelical writers have been active in developing what might be more aptly titled political theology, but it has often remained disconnected from the fundamental theological disciplines of moral theology and/or ethics and systematic theology. Thus, when Ballor argues that Protestant social thought is under serious need of reevaluation and reconstruction, I take him to be saying, at bare minimum, that we must work toward settling on a core biblical motif or theological infrastructure before attempting to resolve specific social and economic questions.

I think holistic biblical stewardship understood as a form of whole-life discipleship may be just the motif or infrastructure that the ecumenical movement has needed "to move purposefully forward." At the beginning of the twenty-first century, an unprecedented opportunity exists to disciple the church in the fundamental biblical pattern of holistic stewardship. As the church becomes increasingly aware of issues of sustainability, seeks to understand and foster the role of business, and expands the message of the grace of giving as a central motif of the Christian life, an environment for personal and corporate transformation takes root.

While most, if not all, Christians employ steward-ship language to describe God's mission in the world, the foundational theological understanding of stewardship varies greatly across denominations and religious traditions. Some groups think stewardship is tithing. Others think stewardship means volunteering or living a simple lifestyle. Still others identify stewardship with environmental conservation, social action, charitable giving, or the making of disciples through evangelism.

Each of these good and necessary activities point to an es-sential facet of stewardship, but each, on its own, falls short of capturing the inspiring vision of biblical stewardship as a form of whole-life discipleship that embraces every legitimate vocation and calling to fulfill God's mission in the world. In this sense, holistic stewardship, transformational generosity, workplace ministry, business as mission, and the theology of work movement all share a common point of origin in the biblical view of mission as whole-life discipleship.

Why has this inspiring vision suffered a setback among evangelicals? It was set back for two primary reasons: (1) because evangelicals siphoned off stewardship from a holistic understanding of God's mission in order to raise funds for global missions and the local church in the early twentieth century, and (2) because evangelicals, at the same time, upheld the problematic distinction between clerical vocations and ordinary vocations, which only served to reinforce the age-old wall that had been erected between sacred and secular callings.

In the immediate aftermath of the First International Congress on World Evangelization, John Stott, in his 1975 Oxford lectures entitled *Christian Mission in the Modern World*, pinpointed the theological root cause of the problem. He discerned that evangelicals seemed unable to integrate satisfactorily the Great Commandment (Lev. 19:18) to "love your neighbor as yourself" with the Great Commission (Matt.

28:19) to "go and make disciples of all nations." God's mission, Stott urged in keeping with Matthew 5:13–16 "describes rather everything the church is sent into the world to do. [It] embraces the church's double vocation of service to be 'the salt of the earth' and 'the light of the world'" (pp. 30–31). The whole church has been sent into the world to accomplish this mission, but our capacity to successfully carry out this mission is diminished due to our disunity, disorganization, duplication of efforts, and tightfistedness.

A proper understanding of the scope of God's mission places a stewardship responsibility on every Christian to join with the Son in the power of the Spirit to fulfill the Father's purpose in creation and redemption. At its most basic level, biblical stewardship is holistic and missional, touching every area of life and employing every legitimate vocation in service to Jesus Christ, who is "the firstborn of all creation" and "the head of … the church" (Col. 1:15–20). If ecumenical engagement could be characterized in this way, then the biblical image of disorder, confusion, impiety, and human arrogance displayed at the Tower of Babel, which aptly describes vast stretches of ecumenical activity, would be brought more into line with the true spirit of complete Christian unity (John 17:23).

I want to conclude by quoting from Ballor's concluding remarks, which, it seems to me, represent well the crux of the issues facing the social witness of mainline Protestant ecumenical engagement:

> It is the fervent hope expressed in this critique that the divisive and ideological language of economistic faith all too often expressed in the social witness of the ecumenical movement might be renewed and reformed. Let our confession be not "I follow Marx," or, "I follow Hayek," "I follow Rand," or "I follow Keynes," but rather, together, "We follow Christ" (see 1 Cor. 1:12).

Ultimately our hope for unity lies not in ourselves or in any feeble human efforts, but in the power and providence of God, "who makes both us and you stand firm in Christ" (2 Cor. 1:26 NIV).

Stephen J. Grabill, Ph.D.
Senior Research Scholar in Theology
Acton Institute
General Editor
NIV Stewardship Study Bible

PREFACE

The year 2010 marks a number of important occasions in the life of the contemporary ecumenical movement. Two of the largest mainline ecumenical groups, the Lutheran World Federation (LWF) and the newly formed World Communion of Reformed Churches (WCRC) are holding major assemblies this year. The WCRC in particular is convening a Uniting General Council in Grand Rapids, Michigan, to facilitate the union of two predecessors: the World Alliance of Reformed Churches (WARC) and the Reformed Ecumenical Council (REC). In many ways, the decisions made at this Uniting General Council will set the stage for the future activity of the WCRC. This present work is inspired in large part by the significance of these events.

In the year 2010, we also observe many other noteworthy occasions. For instance, this year marks the seventy-fifth anniversary of the publication of the powerful and challenging essay by the German theologian Dietrich Bonhoeffer, "The Confessing Church and the Ecumenical Movement." This essay serves as a major touchstone for the present study.

Bonhoeffer's question to the ecumenical movement about its ecclesiastical status is as relevant today as it ever was. This year also marks the sixty-fifth anniversary of Bonhoeffer's execution at the Flossenbürg concentration camp. Bonhoeffer's challenge to the ecumenical movement is one that is authenticated by his dedication to the Confessing Church and his sacrifice in defense of his fellowman.

The two other major interlocutors appearing throughout this study, Paul Ramsey and Ernest W. Lefever, are worth reading in their own right. In many ways, this present book is simply an attempt to update the spirit of critique shared by Bonhoeffer, Ramsey, and Lefever. Thus, if all this book does is inspire a few to take up and read the works of these figures, then this publication has accomplished a great deal. The critique traced through these three men is intended to rebuke in love and out of the hope for reform and reconciliation—a hope made even more urgent by the vast potential for good work that the ecumenical movement might do in service of the Christian community. I believe that this ongoing critique, in which the present study participates, embodies the biblical principle: "Better is open rebuke than hidden love" (Prov. 27:5 NIV).

The purpose of this book is certainly not to be the last word on the matter or to confirm those who have abandoned ecumenical work at various levels and with various institutions in their choice. Neither is it intended to substantiate a social quietism that holds the Christian church to have no public responsibility whatsoever beyond a bare proclamation of the gospel. It is intended to clarify our understanding that while economics and politics involve serious moral realities and warrant sustained ethical deliberation, the results of these kinds of endeavors should not be the basis for division within the church. It is indeed a sorry statement on the present state of the Christian church that economic opinions or political allegiances become more definitive of unity than the spiritual

bond shared as followers of Jesus Christ. We should, therefore, cease all ecumenical attempts to anathematize those
who do not wholeheartedly embrace a particular narrative
of economic globalization.

It is my conviction that the realm of Protestant social
thought is under serious need of reevaluation and reconstruction, and that the sources necessary for such work are
becoming more accessible and available to us. This, now more
than ever, substantiates optimism in the pursuit of such a
project. Protestants are increasingly able to know the Bible
better through their engagement with their own traditions
(including those that date back before the sixteenth century).
Indeed, only by knowing where we come from we will be able
to move purposefully forward. I also believe that the ecumenical movement, in one form or another, has an essential role
to play in this.

ACKNOWLEDGMENTS

This book is a project that would not have come to realization without the significant assistance, encouragement, and support offered by many. The Acton Institute for the Study of Religion & Liberty deserves recognition for its support of the project, both by underwriting this book's publication through its administration of the Christian's Library Press imprint, as well as by its ongoing support of my theological and intellectual pursuits. In the former regard, I am also deeply indebted to the legacy of work introduced through the formation of Christian's Library Press by Gerard Berghoef and Lester DeKoster and their families. I have been greatly blessed by their labors.

Special thanks are due to Stephen Grabill, whose encouragement helped to confirm my feelings about the importance of this critical engagement and whose wise words helped me avoid many pitfalls. It is often difficult to discern whether those projects that inspire us to serious work are, in fact, worthy of the effort and not just undertakings of vain fancy. Many other colleagues and friends offered comments on the text and helped sharpen my thinking on these matters through valued conversation. Thanks are especially owed in this regard to Sam Gregg, Kevin Schmiesing, Ray Nothstine, Marc Vander Maas, Brett Elder, John Couretas, Todd Rester, Jonathan Spalink, Kyle Smith, Dariusz Bryćko, and Nathan Jacobs. Victor Claar was gracious enough to provide valuable insight and corrections on the manuscript. Judy Schafer, Jan Ortiz, and Peter Ho did admirable work under trying circumstances and demanding deadlines to create the book itself.

The members of my family deserve special recognition for their forbearance and sacrifices, which have allowed me to pursue this work. My wife, Amy, has done more than could be reasonably expected of any spouse and has done it with grace, beauty, and love. Her proofreading acumen and editorial instincts are superadded gifts. For all this I am forever grateful.

Any remaining errors, omissions, things done wrongly or improperly left undone are my responsibility alone.

1

A CRITICAL ENGAGEMENT

*Is the ecumenical movement, in its
visible representation, a church?*[1]

—Dietrich Bonhoeffer

Every Christian reader of the New Testament has felt discomfort at some level, perhaps shifting uncomfortably, perhaps skipping quickly ahead in the text, or perhaps shedding tears of mourning, when encountering questions like those of the apostle Paul: "Is Christ divided? Was Paul crucified for you? Were you baptized into the name of Paul?" (1 Cor. 1:13 NIV). As our discomfort and Paul's message make clear, the institutional division of the church is a scandal.

Yet it is equally clear that external unity at the expense of truth is no tenable solution. As the German theologian and pastor Dietrich Bonhoeffer expresses the dilemma, "How will unity be possible where claims to final truth are uttered on every side?"[2] It is in the midst of this perennial dilemma facing the Christian churches that the modern ecumenical movement was born in the twentieth century, and it is in this year, the seventy-fifth anniversary of Bonhoeffer's critical engagement of the ecumenical movement, that this study addresses the challenges facing the ecumenical movement today.

The significance of this scandal of division and the potential answers represented by the ecumenical movement are reason enough for Christians to concern themselves with ecclesial unity.[3] Our recognition of the scandal of institutional division requires us to actively seek out solutions, however improbable and however unrealistic. It is at this point, and this point only, that the ecumenical movement bears serious consideration. Groups such as the World Council of Churches (WCC), the newly formed World Communion of Reformed Churches (WCRC), and the Lutheran World Federation (LWF) represent the most significant long-term global and institutional commitment in the last century in addressing the dilemma of Christian disunity.

For mainline Protestant Christianity in particular, these kinds of efforts hold the promise of addressing the ongoing need for the church to come to some kind of consensus on doctrinal and ethical issues. The function of church councils and international synods did not cease to be salutary either with the Great Schism of 1054 A.D. or the Protestant Reformation of the sixteenth century. For those matters that cannot be decided by individual congregations, classes, or denominations, some higher forum for adjudication, or at least advisement and deliberation, is needed.

Protestant churches have little by way of transdenominational authority other than that represented by ecumenical groups. Even today, more than seventy years after the World Council of Churches was founded in 1937, the ecclesiastical authority of the ecumenical movement remains in doubt. It is in recognition of the need, particularly among Protestant churches, for some kind of institutional ecumenical activity that this study engages the ecumenical movement as represented by the Lutheran World Federation, the World Communion of Reformed Churches, and the World Council of Churches.

Having recognized the important role that ecumenical groups might play in Protestant ecclesiology it remains to establish the importance of engaging these particular groups. These three are the largest, the oldest, and together the most representative of the variety of member churches of the ecumenical movement. There are other important groups, both at the national and international levels, but where exhaustive comprehensiveness is not possible, representative sample must suffice, and the LWF, WCRC, and WCC collectively provide a reliable and authoritative index by which to gauge the current state of Christian ecumenism.

The question is: Why a *critical* engagement? We mean this engagement to be *critical* in at least two senses. First, it refers to the critically important place of ecumenical groups in the ecclesiastical structure of the churches, particularly Protestant churches. Second, it refers to the character of this engagement, one that is oriented toward reform of error and correction of defect. The promise represented by the critical place of the ecumenical movement in the first sense requires criticism in the second sense.

This is particularly the case in those areas that the ecumenical movement has increasingly focused on in recent decades, the areas of social ethics and global economics. James M. Gustafson has noted that "pious Protestants can be virulent racists or civil rights activists. They can be militarists or pacifists, socialists or defenders of the free-market system, regardless of what church agencies teach about these matters." On this basis, he has described "the situation of Protestant churches with regard to moral teachings" as being "only a little short of chaos."[4] If this assessment was accurate when written three decades ago, the situation has progressed well beyond chaos in the intervening years.

3

It is precisely on this point—addressing the chaos of contemporary Protestant ethical thought—that the ecumenical movement has been most ineffectual. This is not because of a lack of effort, but rather than curbing the chaos of unbound individual conscience, the ecumenical movement has contributed to the ethical cacophony through a seemingly endless and continuous stream of pronouncements, decisions, sermons, addresses, letters, reports, and confessions. These efforts are misguided in that while they rightly seek to bring the church's moral authority to bear on contemporary issues, they have done so time and again on matters of prudential judgment where diversity of opinion ought to be respected rather than suppressed. Rather than addressing clear areas of morality, ecumenical pronouncements often attempt to make arbitrary conclusions morally binding.

The reason for this lack of ethical leadership has to do with a more fundamental flaw endemic to ecumenical activism. Ineffectual ethical pronouncements by the ecumenical movement are grounded in faulty economic assumptions. This fundamentally flawed relationship between false economic views and unreliable ethical conclusions is one of the most crippling features of the ecumenical movement's impotence to provide authoritative moral guidance. It is particularly at this point that this critical engagement is aimed and is thus a *qualified* engagement. We do not discuss or consider here, for instance, the significant theological work that is being done in the ecumenical movement, including such things as the *Joint Declaration on Justification* by the Lutheran World Federation and the Roman Catholic Church (1999). Neither do we consider the work of the innumerable other ecumenical organizations, both large and small, local, regional, national, and international. Instead, this critical engagement focuses especially on the character of the recent social witness of the mainline ecumenical movement as represented by the LWF, WCRC, and WCC.

Technological innovation, represented most prominently in the ubiquity of Internet discourse and consumption, has combined with a desire for public influence to create a kind of *ecumenical-industrial complex*, made up in great part by the LWF, WCRC, and WCC, in which the ecumenical movement is promoted, through the media and political engagement, as an end in itself rather than as a church in service to others. The institutional ecumenical movement is no quaintly pious gathering of heavenly minded clergy. Increasingly the ecumenical movement represents major institutional investment, manifested by annual budgets totaling hundreds of millions of dollars aimed at influencing global institutions of the highest order.

It is with the unrealized potential of the ecumenical movement to be of service as a church to the Christian community in mind that the critical engagement of this book is undertaken. This is in the same spirit as that identified by Edwin H. Robinson as Bonhoeffer's motivation for his critique of the ecumenical movement in 1935. As Robinson writes of Bonhoeffer, "It was because he had so high a regard for the ecumenical movement that he was constantly examining it and subjecting it [to] searching criticism."[5] However, this service is only possible where the ecumenical movement does identify itself as a church, and so the critical engagement of this book follows in the path preceded by three other significant voices from the past century: Dietrich Bonhoeffer, Paul Ramsey, and Ernest W. Lefever.

Bonhoeffer: The Confessing Church and the Ecumenical Movement (1935)

Dietrich Bonhoeffer (1906–1945) was a theologian and pastor intimately involved in the German church struggle (*Kirchenkampf*)—the attempt by the Third Reich to consolidate control under a central Reich bishop and promote pro-Nazi sentiment in the German church.[6] Born in Breslau (now Wrocław, Poland), Bonhoeffer committed at an early age to the study of theology and quickly was recognized for his academic acumen. He achieved the licentiate degree in 1927 for a dissertation completed under Reinhold Seeberg, and he successfully defended his *Habilitationsschrift* in 1930, a remarkable achievement for a twenty-four-year-old.[7] Bonhoeffer's engagement with the ecumenical movement grows out of his participation in the church struggle, particularly the fight against the imposition of the Aryan clauses on the church, which would prohibit non-Aryans (e.g., Jews) from authorized ministry.[8]

Christ existing for others is the basic definition given by Bonhoeffer of the church, which he believes to be the fundamental sociological reality in the world.[9] It is with this sense of the church in mind that Bonhoeffer issues his critique of the ecumenical movement in the form of an essay, "The Confessing Church and the Ecumenical Movement."[10] As we shall see, the challenging question articulated in 1935, "Is the ecumenical movement, in its visible representation, a church?" echoes throughout the history of the movement.[11] Despite the span of the intervening decades and the attempts to come to grips with Bonhoeffer's challenge, the ecumenical movement still has not been able to answer this question definitively.

There are many reasons for this ambiguity. In part, the questionable status of the ecumenical movement is simply a corporate expression of the existential uncertainty that faces all individual Christians. This question to the ecumenical movement is a form of the basic question of Christian existence, also articulated by Bonhoeffer: "Who is Jesus Christ, for us, today?"[12] Bonhoeffer understood that in this fundamental point of departure, in the answer to this basic question, the validity of ecumenical endeavor hangs in the balance. Thus, he asks, "Is the ecumenical movement, in its visible representation, a church? Or, to put it the other way round: Has the real ecumenicity of the church as witnessed in the New Testament found visible and appropriate expression in the ecumenical organization?"[13] This is, he realizes, "the question of the authority with which the ecumenical movement speaks and acts."[14]

If the ecumenical movement is a church, then its existence is not ultimately founded on human work but instead is based upon the work of the Spirit of God. In this way, "If the ecumenical movement claims to be the church of Christ, it is as imperishable as the church of Christ itself; in that case its work has ultimate importance and ultimate authority."[15] An affirmative answer to the question of the ecumenical movement's status as church articulates the highest possible view of the importance of the movement and its place in the Christian church and the larger world.

Nevertheless, notes Bonhoeffer, "There is evidently the possibility of not understanding the ecumenical movement in its present visible form as a church."[16] This alternative would be what in the Reformed view is distinguished from the church as institution, that is, the church as organism.[17] As Bonhoeffer puts it, the ecumenical movement "could indeed be an association of Christian men of whom each was rooted in his own church and who now assemble either for common tactical and practical action or for unauthoritative theological conversation with one another."[18] In this case, however, the ecumenical movement would lose any special claims to theological or moral authority.

It would instead become a worldly institution like any other, one that happens to be made up of professing Christians that would rely on worldly criteria for expertise, judgment, and authority. Any action by such a group "might have only a neutral character, not involving any confession, and this conversation might only have the informative character of a discussion, without including a judgement or even a decision on this or that doctrine, or even church."[19] It would be a place for discussion but not decision, dialogue but not determination.

For Bonhoeffer, the confession is a key characteristic of the ecumenical movement as church rather than as association. Bonhoeffer calls "the living confession" the "only weapon" of the church, a weapon that "does not shatter."[20] It is within the context of this call to confession that Bonhoeffer emphasizes the importance of truth claims, for "where one church by itself seeks unity with another church, leaving aside any claim to truth, the truth is denied and the church has surrendered itself."[21] In order for the ecumenical movement to truly be a church, it must confess itself to be sinful and broken, completely dependent on Christ, committed to him and opposed to his enemies.

What this confession requires concretely will differ in each particular context. In the case of Bonhoeffer, he is at pains to make the case that the German church's struggle of the 1930s provides the fundamental challenge to the ecumenical movement, the crisis to which it must respond with a clear Yes or No. In Bonhoeffer's view, "the German church struggle marks the second great stage in the history of the ecumenical movement and will in a decisive way be normative for its future."[22] As to the question of the status of the Confessing Church and the German Christian Church, in order to be a church, the ecumenical movement must make a confession for one and against the other.

In our contemporary setting, the contrast between these two options would be between a church that relies on its confession and an activist group that relies on its expertise or simply provides a forum for open-ended dialogue. For Bonhoeffer the choice is clear. Either the ecumenical movement is an institutional form of the Christian church, or it abandons any special claims to authority, and, in so doing, undermines its own validity. Bonhoeffer's critique of the ecumenical movement is in the broadest sense an *ecclesiastical* concern.

Ramsey: Who Speaks for the Church? (1967)

Paul Ramsey (1913–1988) was an American Protestant theological ethicist. Ramsey taught religion and ethics at Princeton University for the better part of four decades, and published widely and influentially on a variety of general and specialized ethical topics.[23] The Anglican ethicist Oliver O'Donovan has described Ramsey as "an ecumenically eclectic Western Christian moralist."[24] O'Donovan traces the vigor that characterizes Ramsey's career and the commitment to engage pressing public issues that motivated much of his work. O'Donovan writes that "Ramsey had an insatiable appetite for charting the unheard-of dilemmas which the new age was producing and a solid confidence in the power of Christian wisdom to illuminate them."[25]

In 1967, Paul Ramsey turned his attention to the ecumenical movement, exploring the processes and deliberations of the previous year's Geneva Conference on Church and Society of the World Council of Churches.[26] In his critique of the conference, Ramsey articulates and expands on concerns similar to those raised by Bonhoeffer's basic question over thirty years before. In Ramsey's analysis, the ecumenical movement has largely abandoned the proper work of the institutional church and engaged in a program of political and social activism. Where Bonhoeffer had asked whether it was the authority of the church "with which the ecumenical movement speaks and acts," Ramsey asks whether or not the ecumenical movement "speaks for the church."[27]

It is clear to Ramsey that the ecumenical movement at least intends to speak for the church, and rightly so. Ramsey concurs with Bonhoeffer that the ecumenical movement only functions positively when it understands itself to be an institutional form of the church and acts in appropriate fashion. Thus, writes, Ramsey, "an ecumenical Christian ethics must be the clarification of the message of the church concerning

9

the meaning of Christian life in the contemporary world."[28] If, however, the ecumenical movement is attempting to function as a church, and is right in doing so, what then is the focus of Ramsey's complaint?

Throughout his critique Ramsey employs the terms *social action curia* and *Church and Society syndrome*, by which he means to describe "the passion for numerous particular pronouncements on policy questions to the consequent neglect of basic decision- and action-oriented principles of ethical and political analysis."[29] In Ramsey's view, the trend in ecumenical ethical thought has been to attempt to speak authoritatively and concretely on specific policies, particularly on topics in which there is no clear moral, Christian, or biblical mandate. Ramsey contends:

> Of late, however, ecumenical social action pronouncements have presumed to encompass the prudence of churchmen in their capacities as citizens. It has been easier to arrive at specific recommendations and condemnations after inadequate deliberation than to penetrate to a deeper and deeper level the meaning of Christian responsibility—leaving to the conscience of individuals and groups of individuals both the task and the freedom to arrive at specific conclusions through untrammeled debate about particular social policies.[30]

Ramsey's words, first written over forty years ago, capture the spirit of the ecumenical movement's ethical teaching in the intervening decades.

The problem is not that the ecumenical movement presumes to speak for the church but rather that it presumes to speak for the church on such issues and in such a way that tyrannizes necessary ethical deliberation, both individual and communal. As Ramsey writes, "the specific solution of urgent problems is the work of political prudence and worldly wisdom. In this there is room for legitimate disagreement among Christians and among other people as well in the public domain—which disagreement ought to be welcomed and not led one way toward specific conclusions."[31] The confusion here is between ethics and economics, between moral mandates and political prudence.

Recognition of the gap between these realities is critical for authentic ecumenical ethical discourse. "However great the overlap in particular instances," contends Ramsey, "there are nonetheless vital distinctions to be made between Christian moral judgments on the one hand and particular political, legal, and military judgments on the other; or between what is morally permitted or prohibited and what is tactically or prudentially advisable and practicable."[32]

In Ramsey's view, the ecumenical hubris to speak authoritatively on particular political matters and policies stems from a misunderstanding of the role of the institutional church in society. "One cannot have it both ways," says Ramsey, "by declaring that we have taken our exodus from 'Christendom' while continuing to fashion Christian social ethics in the manner of the great cultural churches of the past."[33] The ecumenical movement, in its endless pronouncements on this or that policy, presumes a place of prestige and authority akin to that enjoyed by the church in the premodern era. Ramsey thus identifies the ecumenical movement with what he calls a "cultural church," a church that attempts to use its authority and station to influence secular political power in a manner consistent with privileged secular advocacy.[34]

Ramsey places himself in dialogue with the discussion raised classically by H. Richard Niebuhr's *Christ and Culture* (1951).[35] Niebuhr's fivefold typology of the varieties of Christian interaction with culture has sparked a long and fruitful dialogue about the validity of such schemes, but here Ramsey is in some sense invoking the long history of the relationship between the Christian church and culture.[36] Ramsey writes, "The oddity is that contemporary ecumenical social ethics evidences less acknowledgment of the separation between the church and the office of magistrate or citizen than was clearly acknowledged by the great cultural churches of the past."[37] In a way akin to the privilege enjoyed by a Constantinian form of the church, the ecumenical movement attempts to influence national and transnational politics, speaking from a position of presumed spiritual authority.

In this context, claims Ramsey, "The church becomes a *secular* 'sect' in its ecumenical ethics set over against the world as it is, instead of becoming truly a Christian sect concerned to nurture a distinctive ethos set over against an acculturated Christianity or against a culture that is no longer Christendom."[38] In reducing its witness to advocacy for a particular set of policies, the ecumenical movement has abandoned the attempt to proclaim the gospel, the true foundation of its spiritual authority. "This is surely a form of culture-Christianity," writes Ramsey, "even if it is not that of the great cultural churches of the past. This is, indeed, the most barefaced sectarianism and but a new form of culture-Christianity. It would identify Christianity with the cultural vitalities, with the movement of history, with where the action is, with the next and even now the real establishment, but not with the present hollow forms."[39] In this way, the question of how the church's prophetic responsibility ought to be expressed in a post-Christendom era has not received adequate attention from the ecumenical movement. Instead, it has simply assumed that the same form of prophetic pronouncement is as appropriate today as it was in the era of the Reformation, the medieval church, or the Old Testament monarchy.

Bonhoeffer's critique includes guarded optimism about the ecumenical movement's potential for confessionally grounded engagement with the world. In Ramsey's view, this optimism has given way to criticism of the presumptive cooption of secular social policy by the ecumenical movement's "social action curia." As the ecumenical movement progresses from infancy to maturity between 1935 and 1967, the critique has sharpened and taken on a more specific shape. In this way, Ramsey's critique is a narrowing of Bonhoeffer's ecclesiastical concern to a more specific *ethical* complaint.

Lefever: Amsterdam to Nairobi, Nairobi to Vancouver (1949–1987)

Ernest W. Lefever (1919–2009) was a Protestant theologian, ethicist, and political intellectual, educated with a doctorate in Christian ethics from Yale University. He began his career in the world of public policy as a Senior Fellow at the Brookings Institution in 1964. In 1976, Lefever founded the Ethics and Public Policy Center (EPPC), where he served as president until his retirement in 1989. Lefever's vision for the EPPC was threefold: "First, EPPC sought to bring reasoned debate to those controversial issues of the day that had been monopolized by single-issue groups; that is it strove to enrich the moral and political debate by drawing on wisdom across the ideological spectrum." In addition, "the center sought to analyze those issues against the background of long-standing Western concepts and values, and therefore, to clarify the relationship between political necessity and moral principle." And third, the "EPPC's belief in the crucial role of religion in American society addressed a moral, cultural, and political factor usually neglected by most secular research organizations."[40]

Lefever became acquainted with the ecumenical movement during his work with the War Prisoners' Aid of the World's YMCA in Britain and West Germany between 1945–1948, as well as during his service from 1952–1954 as associate director of international affairs with the U.S. National Council of Churches.[41] Lefever's primary mature engagement with the ecumenical movement comes in the form of two books written over the span of a decade. In 1979, Lefever's *Amsterdam to*

Nairobi: The World Council of Churches and the Third World
criticizes the Council's increasing embrace of the perspective
of liberation theology. As he summarizes, "There is ample
evidence for concern about the deep and widespread impact
of the Marxist interpretation of history and strategy for change
within WCC circles and among liberal Christians generally."[42]
Here, Lefever's critical engagement embraces the questions
about the ecclesiastical status and the political identification
raised previously by Bonhoeffer and Ramsey and adds to them
the concern that a specific ideology has negatively influenced
the ecumenical movement.

Lefever's analysis focuses on these kinds of questions: "*For*
whom does the WCC speak? Does it speak and act for the
member churches? Or, does it speak and act only for itself?
To whom does the Council speak? Does it speak only to the
churches and individual Christians, or also to governments
and to the world?"[43] This is an extension of that critique
raised by Bonhoeffer: whether the WCC identifies itself as a
church institution and claims to speak officially on behalf of
the church. Bonhoeffer, Ramsey, and Lefever concur that the
only way in which the words and actions of the ecumenical
movement make sense is if they are understood to be representing in some institutional way the church's witness to
itself and to the world.

Picking up explicitly on a major aspect of Ramsey's critique,
Lefever cites the propensity for the WCC to too closely align
itself with particular political interests, short-circuiting necessary debate and taking on the stance of political activism
rather than ecclesiastical witness. Thus, says Lefever, "It is
dangerous for any Christian body to identify itself fully with
any specific political cause or order, whether the prevailing
one or a challenge to it. In identifying with a secular power
or agency, the church runs the risk of losing its critical dis-
tance and of subverting its prophetic function, its capacity to
judge all movements and systems by universal Christian stan-

dards."[44] Instead, as Lefever writes, "Pronouncements should emerge from an intensive dialogue that seeks to discover the implications of the Christian gospel for the particular social or political issue addressed. This dialogue must be true to the theological and social teachings of the churches and must take into account the facts of the situation." Extensive dialogue is a critical component of authentic ecumenical action: "In short, church pronouncements should be morally sound and empirically informed if they are to be politically relevant."[45]

Undermining this kind of necessary dialogue, however, is the presence of an ideology that excludes debate and democratic representation of a diversity of political perspectives and vilifies alternative views. Key to this kind of tyranny of dialogue is what Lefever calls the "social-action establishment," echoing Ramsey's critique of the "social action curia" involved in governing the WCC. Thus, writes Lefever, those involved in the administration of the WCC at the highest levels tend to share a basic ideological perspective. There is, in short, a kind of "echo chamber" effect, in which institutional bureaucrats and management attract and employ those who are in essential agreement about the problems and solutions facing the world. In this way, ideological unity trumps true ecclesiastical catholicity.

At this point, Lefever still sees room for substantive engagement of the WCC and attempts to correct the ecumenical movement's defects. To this end, he makes a number of particular recommendations specifically focused on those problems he has identified in the Council's adoption of the perspective of liberation theology. In the case of ideological unanimity, for instance, Lefever writes that "an effort should be made to recruit a headquarters staff more varied in theological, ethical, and political outlook. The social-action establishment has often been more eager to talk to Marxists than to conservative evangelical Christians."[46] Calling this a "sad irony," Lefever recognizes that if anything undermines the authenticity of ecumenical unity, it is the closer identification of worldly bonds (whether political, social, tribal, ethnic, familial, economic, or otherwise) than of spiritual bonds in Christ.[47]

This has become a feature of contemporary Christianity at least in the North American context, and represents what Edward Norman sees as the conflation of religion with morality, in which the two are "assumed to be virtually interchangeable terms."[48] If political perspective is equated with morality, then unity of partisan politics becomes much more determinative of fellowship than ecclesiastical unity, and it explains why there is so much cross-confessional and interreligious ecumenical action drawn largely along partisan political lines.[49]

By the time Lefever writes a follow-up volume in 1987, *Nairobi to Vancouver: The World Council of Churches and the World, 1975–87*, he is much more pessimistic about the likelihood of reform within the WCC. The second volume overlaps with the first and raises many of the same complaints. What is significant about the difference in perspective between the two books is that Lefever sees much less hope of reformation of the ecumenical movement. In his view, the neo-Marxist liberationist theological ideology, which Lefever had previously identified as gaining ascendancy in the WCC, now has become much more pervasive and influential. In this latter volume, Lefever presses even more pointedly an aspect of the critique on the economic question raised in passing earlier.[50]

As he writes in 1979, "The liberation theologians also underestimate the values of a market economy over a Marxist or socialist economy. They have refused to accept the fact that market economies with minimal government restrictions have demonstrated far greater capacity to produce and distribute goods and services than Marxist and other government-controlled economies."[51] Indeed, says Lefever, the liberation theologians "tend to accept the neo-Marxist myth that colonialism, neocolonialism, and transnational

corporations are the causes of poverty in the Third World."⁵²
While this element is present in the ecumenical movement
in 1979, Lefever finds that it has gained supreme dominance
less than a decade later.

Thus, in 1987, Lefever concludes: "For the past decade
and more, the leaders of the World Council of Churches have
addressed selective aspects of the economic question, almost
exclusively from an ideological perspective that asserts the
superiority of a government-administered economy over the
market. The Council's pronouncements assume a cause-effect
relationship between Western capitalism and imperialism on
the one hand, and poverty, oppression, and militarism on the
other."⁵³ Here, the question of economic ideology has taken
center stage in the ongoing critique of the ecumenical movement. Lefever's *economic* critique is a further narrowing of
Ramsey's ethical complaint (which is itself in turn a narrowing
of Bonhoeffer's ecclesiastical concern).

Summary

Does the ecumenical movement represent an institutional
form of the church, or does it not? asks Dietrich Bonhoeffer
in his provocative essay, "The Confessing Church and the
Ecumenical Movement." Despite decades of effort and toil,
the ecumenical movement has continued to founder on this
basic question of ecclesiastical status for reasons beyond the
unavoidable ambiguity endemic to Christian life on this side
of glory.

One basic problem with an affirmative answer to Bonhoeffer's question is that the ecumenical movement, especially within the last half-century, has often not behaved as
an institutional form of the church ought. It has not been
appropriately circumspect in its ethical pronouncements on
specific matters of public policy. It has not been careful to be
true to the honest variety of opinion that exists within the

Christian community. As Ramsey says of ecumenical social ethics, "the *abusus* (policy-directives) has become *usus*—it has become the fashion—and that one will not sense the strength of the case for radical reformation in the aims of church social teachings unless he begins by acknowledging this to be true."[54] Whether the ecumenical movement is an institutional form of the church in any traditional sense, or whether it is a kind of advocacy group that achieves authority only by means of a kind of special pleading for the Christian church's influence on society, remains unclear given the abuse of ecumenical social ethical discourse.

Indeed, by the time Lefever writes his critical engagement with the ecumenical movement, this propensity for specific policy pronouncement has taken firm root but has also done so in a pointedly ideological manner. The ecumenical movement has confused the descriptive social science of economics with the normative claims of Christian ethics. Even more, it has taken a particular economic perspective and totalized its claims within Christian ethics, providing a basically neo-Marxist narrative, worldview (*Weltanschauung*), and ideology as foundational. As Lefever writes, the ecumenical movement favors one of the two basic approaches to economics. This perspective "emphasizes fidelity to an ideology—a world-view—that seeks to explain what is wrong with an existing system and how it could be improved or replaced."[55] He finds that in WCC engagement of social questions between the early 1970s and late 1980s, "there was rough underlying consistency rooted in a shared revolutionary worldview."[56] In the ecumenical world, economic narrative has become identical to ethical imperative, and deviation from this whole-cloth worldview is anathema. If we follow Norman's diagnosis that religion and morality have become conflated, the further conflation of ethics and economics is especially disturbing. Religion in large part now consists in an economic worldview, with ethics as the middle term.

This brief study explores some of the more mundane reasons for the ambiguity about the ecclesiastical, ethical, and economic status of the ecumenical movement and its authority. On the one hand, this book serves as a kind of basic introduction to the world of contemporary ecumenical social thought in its various institutional expressions (e.g., LWF, WCRC, WCC). It also introduces and updates a significant line of critical engagement with the ecumenical movement in its various individual expressions (i.e., Bonhoeffer, Ramsey, Lefever).

On the basis of this twofold endeavor, this study finds that the basic line of criticism holds true today and that the flaws of the ecumenical movement's social teaching have become more pronounced in the intervening decades. A significant new aspect of this is the ecumenical movement's overwhelming focus on addressing the world and its powers directly by attempting to influence global and national politics through the union of ecclesiastical status and media personalities. The message coming out of the ecumenical movement on ethical and economic matters is increasingly univocal, regardless of particular confessional tradition or ecclesiastical heritage. Indeed, the dominant characteristic of economic ecumenical engagement is the rejection of the neoliberal paradigm. Shorthand for this union is the term *ecumenical-industrial complex*, the cross-institutional emphasis on public engagement and political advocacy of a particular economic ideology through the mainstream media and channels of influence.

A basic assumption of this study is that some form of ecumenical engagement is a nonnegotiable for churches today.[57] Whatever their shortcomings, the institutions that make up the mainline ecumenical movement, the Lutheran World Federation, the World Communion of Reformed Churches, and the World Council of Churches, represent a significant and undisputed place of prominence in the ecumenical world. In introducing ecumenical social thought as well as this

19

particular line of critical engagement, the hope is that a dialogue can be entered into that focuses on the reformation of the defects of the ecumenical movement, particularly in the areas of ethical and economic thought.

To realize these purposes, this study examines in turn representative statements and documents from the major ecumenical bodies. Each chapter devoted to the LWF, WCRC, and WCC in turn will provide a brief background and history of the organization in general as well as of the particular documents under examination.[58] These documents have been selected for their timeliness so that some of the most recent statements available will be examined. They have also been selected for their authority; the emphasis will be on those documents of a more authoritative character than those of a more transitory or passing nature.[59] This will be followed by a summary of the main points of the document that touch on matters of ethics and economics. The chapters will conclude with a critical analysis of these points, which seeks to highlight the positive aspects of these documents as well as their shortcomings, while also providing corrective resources from alternative viewpoints.[60] The concluding chapter will summarize a number of basic concepts and suggestions that could substantively improve the character of the ecumenical social witness.

One biblical image for disunity is the Tower of Babel: "So the Lord scattered them from there over all the earth, and they stopped building the city. That is why it was called Babel—because there the Lord confused the language of the whole world. From there the Lord scattered them over the face of the whole earth" (Gen. 11:8–9 NIV). Even so, there is hope that the language spoken so often today in the ecumenical movement, the language of neo-Marxist liberation, can be corrected and brought successfully into dialogue with that of the main Christian tradition.[61] What may be impossible for human beings is not impossible for God (Matt. 19:26).

Notes

1. Dietrich Bonhoeffer, "The Confessing Church and the Ecumenical Movement," in *No Rusty Swords: Letters, Lectures and Notes 1928–1936*, trans. Edwin H. Robertson and John Bowden, ed. Edwin H. Robertson (New York: Harper & Row, 1965), 330.

2. Bonhoeffer, "The Confessing Church and the Ecumenical Movement," 336.

3. For a basic primer, see Thomas E. FitzGerald, *The Ecumenical Movement: An Introductory History* (Westport: Praeger, 2004).

4. James M. Gustafson, *Protestant and Roman Catholic Ethics: Prospects for Rapprochement* (Chicago: University of Chicago Press, 1980), 130.

5. See Bonhoeffer, "The Confessing Church and the Ecumenical Movement," 325.

6. The best biographical source on Bonhoeffer remains the massive study by his friend Eberhard Bethge, *Dietrich Bonhoeffer: A Biography*, rev. ed., trans. Eric Mosbacher et al. (Minneapolis: Fortress Press, 2000). For Bonhoeffer's early engagement with the ecumenical movement, see especially pages 238–56. More recently, see also Eric Metaxas, *Bonhoeffer: Pastor, Martyr, Prophet, Spy* (Nashville: Thomas Nelson, 2010), 217–20.

7. Bonhoeffer's first dissertation is available in English translation as *Sanctorum Communio: A Theological Study of the Sociology of the Church*, trans. Reinhard Krauss and Nancy Lukens, ed. Clifford J. Green, Dietrich Bonhoeffer Works 1 (Minneapolis: Fortress Press, 1998). Bonhoeffer's *Habilitationsschift* in English translation is *Act and Being: Transcendental Philosophy and Ontology in Systematic Theology*, trans. H. Martin Rumscheidt, ed. Wayne Whitson Floyd Jr., Dietrich Bonhoeffer Works 2 (Minneapolis: Fortress Press, 1996).

8. For more on Bonhoeffer's view of the ecumenical movement in relation to the church struggle and the Confessing Church, see Jordan J. Ballor, "The Aryan Clause, the Confessing Church, and

the Ecumenical Movement: Barth and Bonhoeffer on Natural Theology, 1933–1935," *Scottish Journal of Theology* 59, no. 3 (August 2006): 263–80.

9. See for instance, Bonhoeffer, *Sanctorum Communio*, 188; and also Clifford J. Green, *Bonhoeffer: A Theology of Sociality* (Grand Rapids: Eerdmans, 1999).

10. Dietrich Bonhoeffer, "The Confessing Church and the Ecumenical Movement," 326–44. The essay is reprinted in *Dietrich Bonhoeffer: Witness to Jesus Christ*, ed. John W. de Gruchy (Minneapolis: Fortress Press, 1991), 134–48.

11. Bonhoeffer, "The Confessing Church and the Ecumenical Movement," 330. For Bonhoeffer's influence and the history of the church in East Germany following World War II, as well as more recent ecumenical relationships, see Gregory Baum, *The Church for Others: Protestant Theology in Communist East Germany* (Grand Rapids: Eerdmans, 1996).

12. For an exploration of this theme in Bonhoeffer's thought, in which it is asserted that the question "forms the cantus firmus of Bonhoeffer's theological development from the beginning to the end," see Andreas Pangritz, "Who Is Jesus Christ, for Us, Today?" in *Cambridge Companion to Dietrich Bonhoeffer*, ed. John W. de Gruchy (New York: Cambridge University Press), 134.

13. Bonhoeffer, "The Confessing Church and the Ecumenical Movement," 330.

14. Bonhoeffer, "The Confessing Church and the Ecumenical Movement," 330.

15. Bonhoeffer, "The Confessing Church and the Ecumenical Movement," 331.

16. Bonhoeffer, "The Confessing Church and the Ecumenical Movement," 331.

17. On this distinction, see Louis Berkhof, *Systematic Theology* (Grand Rapids: Eerdmans, 1998), 567. For a fuller treatment,

see Herman Bavinck, *Reformed Dogmatics*, Vol. 4, *Holy Spirit, Church, and New Creation*, trans. John Vriend, ed. John Bolt (Grand Rapids: Baker Academic, 2008), 329–32. For the relevance of the distinction with regard to social matters, see Calvin P. Van Reken, "The Church's Role in Social Justice," *Calvin Theological Journal* 34, no. 1 (April 1999): 198–202.

18. Bonhoeffer, "The Confessing Church and the Ecumenical Movement," 331.

19. Bonhoeffer, "The Confessing Church and the Ecumenical Movement," 331–32. Contrast for instance the view that locates authority solely in the local church, relegating synods or councils to an advisory role, as expressed by the Lutheran John T. Mueller, *Christian Dogmatics* (St. Louis: Concordia, 1934), 561: "Neither individual persons (Popes, princes, presidents) nor assemblies (church councils, synods, pastoral conferences, parliaments, consistories) have been ordained by our Lord to decide questions of faith or church polity." For a helpful survey of various perspectives on the church, see Avery Dulles, *Models of the Church*, expanded ed. (New York: Image, 2000), particularly chapter 2, "The Church as Institution," 26–38.

20. Bonhoeffer, "The Confessing Church and the Ecumenical Movement," 338, 336.

21. Bonhoeffer, "The Confessing Church and the Ecumenical Movement," 336.

22. Bonhoeffer, "The Confessing Church and the Ecumenical Movement," 326.

23. Paul Ramsey, *The Essential Paul Ramsey: A Collection*, ed. William Werpehowski and Stephen D. Crocco (New Haven: Yale University Press, 1994). See also James Turner Johnson, *Love and Society: Essays in the Ethics of Paul Ramsey* (Missoula: Scholars Press, 1975).

24. Oliver O'Donovan, "Obituary: Paul Ramsey (1913–1988)," *Studies in Christian Ethics* 1, no. 1 (1988): 84.

25. O'Donovan, "Obituary: Paul Ramsey (1913–1988)," 82.

26. Paul Ramsey, *Who Speaks for the Church? A Critique of the 1966 Geneva Conference on Church and Society* (Nashville: Abingdon Press, 1967).

27. Bonhoeffer, "The Confessing Church and the Ecumenical Movement," 330; Ramsey, *Who Speaks for the Church?* 26–28.

28. Ramsey, *Who Speaks for the Church?* 16.

29. Ramsey, *Who Speaks for the Church?* 13.

30. Ramsey, *Who Speaks for the Church?* 15.

31. Ramsey, *Who Speaks for the Church?* 19.

32. Ramsey, *Who Speaks for the Church?* 53.

33. Ramsey, *Who Speaks for the Church?* 20.

34. See Ramsey, *Who Speaks for the Church?* 50: "The peril that stands close to the elbow is that we turn the church inside out and render it entirely congruent with secular decision making, abolishing all distinction between the temporal and the spiritual power in the content of ecumenical ethics."

35. H. Richard Niebuhr, *Christ and Culture* (New York: Harper, 1951).

36. Significant here are the alternative typologies proposed by Baltzell and Carter, which distinguish between Constantinian, Christendom, or magisterial approaches (Puritan) and non-Christendom views, such as those of the Anabapists and radical reformers (Quaker). See E. Digby Baltzell, *Puritan Boston and Quaker Philadelphia: Two Protestant Ethics and the Spirit of Class Authority and Leadership* (New York: Free Press, 1979); and Craig A. Carter, *Rethinking Christ and Culture: A Post-Christendom Perspective* (Grand Rapids: Brazos Press, 2006). See also Lawrence W. Sherman, "Two Protestant Ethics and the Spirit of the Reformation," in *Restorative Justice and Civil Society*, ed. Heather Strang and John Braithwaite (New York: Cambridge University Press, 2001), 35–55.

37. Ramsey, *Who Speaks for the Church?* 20. Here Ramsey makes specific reference to the fourteenth-century papal bull *Unam Sanctam.*

38. Ramsey, *Who Speaks for the Church?* 55. On contemporary questions about religion in the public square, see Hunter Baker, *The End of Secularism* (Wheaton: Crossway, 2009).

39. Ramsey, *Who Speaks for the Church?* 55.

40. William M. Brailsford, "Ethics and Public Policy Center," in *American Conservatism: An Encyclopedia*, ed. Bruce Frohnen, Jeremy Beer, and Jeffery O. Nelson (Wilmington: ISI Books, 2006), 284.

41. Ernest W. Lefever, *Amsterdam to Nairobi: The World Council of Churches and the Third World* (Washington, D.C.: Ethics and Public Policy Center, 1979), xi–xii. Lefever was also in attendance at the WCC assemblies in Amsterdam (1948) and Evanston (1954).

42. Ernest W. Lefever, *Amsterdam to Nairobi*, 51. For the juxtaposition of Christianity and liberalism as competing religions, see J. Gresham Machen, *Christianity and Liberalism* (Grand Rapids: Eerdmans, 1923). For the juxtaposition of Christianity and Communism as competing religions, see Lester DeKoster, *Communism and Christian Faith* (Grand Rapids: Eerdmans, 1962). See also J. A. Emerson Vermaat, *The World Council of Churches and Politics, 1975–1986* (Lanham: Freedom House, 1989); and Edward Norman, *Christianity and the World Order* (New York: Oxford University Press, 1979).

43. Lefever, *Amsterdam to Nairobi*, 9.

44. Lefever, *Amsterdam to Nairobi*, 4–5.

45. Lefever, *Amsterdam to Nairobi*, 4.

46. Lefever, *Amsterdam to Nairobi*, 57.

47. Compare, for instance, the criticism of the German Christian perspective in a church election pamphlet drafted by Franz Hildebrandt, in *No Rusty Swords*, 210: "The German Christians say: A godless fellow-countryman is nearer to us than one of another race, even if he sings the same hymn or prays the same prayer (Hossenfelder, Hamburg). The Bible says: Whoever does the will of God is my brother, and sister, and mother (Mark 3:35)." Compare also the contention of John W. de Gruchy, *Confessions of a Christian Humanist* (Minneapolis: Fortress Press, 2006), 100: "There is sometimes more uniting such believers and non-believers than there is uniting believers with some kinds of religious people, or uniting such secular neo-humanists with self-centered secularists."

48. Edward Norman, foreword to *Nairobi to Vancouver: The World Council of Churches and the World, 1975–87*, by Ernest W. Lefever (Washington, D.C.: Ethics and Public Policy Center, 1987), ix.

49. It would be fruitful on this point to explore the social sources of ecumenism, akin to the kind of work done by H. Richard Niebuhr, *The Social Sources of Denominationalism* (New York: Henry Holt and Co., 1929).

50. Lefever's critique is surveyed by Martin Conway, "Under Public Scrutiny," in *A History of the Ecumenical Movement, 1968–2000*, vol. 3, ed. John Briggs, Mercy Amba Oduyoye, and Georges Tsetsis (Geneva: World Council of Churches, 2004), 438–440. Conway writes that the kind of criticism he detects in Lefever's work "has been a considerable burden to leaders of the WCC member churches in the US and beyond" (440). At the same time, however, Conway admits, "Where there is no criticism, there will be no movement" (453).

51. Lefever, *Amsterdam to Nairobi*, 52.

52. Lefever, *Amsterdam to Nairobi*, 52.

53. Lefever, *Nairobi to Vancouver*, 56.

54. Ramsey, *Who Speaks for the Church?* 17.

55. Lefever, *Nairobi to Vancouver*, 56.

56. Lefever, *Nairobi to Vancouver*, 78.

57. Indeed, some churches are institutionally mandated to partici-
pate in such activities. For the Christian Reformed Church, see
"Reformed Ecumenical Councils," in *Church Order and Rules for
Synodical Procedure 2009* (Grand Rapids: Christian Reformed
Church, 2009), II.D.50.a, p. 81: "Synod shall send delegates to
Reformed ecumenical synods in which the Christian Reformed
Church cooperates with other denominations which confess
and maintain the Reformed faith." See also Henry Zwaanstra,
*Catholicity and Secession: A Study of Ecumenicity in the Christian
Reformed Church* (Grand Rapids: Eerdmans, 1991).

58. For the Lutheran World Federation, *Communion, Responsibil-
ity, Accountability: Responding as a Lutheran Communion to
Neoliberal Globalization*, ed. Karen L. Bloomquist (Geneva:
Lutheran World Federation, 2004); for the WCRC, *The Accra
Confession: Covenanting for Justice in the Economy and the
Earth* (Accra: World Alliance of Reformed Churches, 2004);
and for the WCC, *Report from the Public Issues Committee*,
Ninth General Assembly, Porto Alegre, Brazil (February 23,
2006).

59. This attempts to mirror Lefever's method for engaging the
WCC. See Lefever, *Amsterdam to Nairobi*, 7: "The World
Council speaks with different levels of authority and degrees
of consensus."

60. Major dialogue partners here will include Victor V. Claar and
Robin J. Klay, *Economics in Christian Perspective: Theory, Policy and Life Choices* (Downers Grove: InterVarsity Press, IVP
Academic, 2007); Samuel J. Gregg, *Economic Thinking for the
Theologically Minded* (Lanham: University Press of America,
2001); John R. Schneider, *The Good of Affluence: Seeking God
in a Culture of Wealth* (Grand Rapids: Eerdmans, 2002).

61. Compare Norman, *Christianity and the World Order*, 15. See also Lefever, *Amsterdam to Nairobi*, 48. As Thomas Aquinas, a representative of this "classical Christian tradition," puts it, there is basis for hopeful dialogue with those who agree with the divine authority of the Bible. See Aquinas, *Summa Theologica* (New York: Benzinger Bros., 1948), P.1, Q.1, A.8: "Hence Sacred Scripture, since it has no science above itself, can dispute with one who denies its principles only if the opponent admits some at least of the truths obtained through divine revelation; thus we can argue with heretics from texts in Holy Writ, and against those who deny one article of faith, we can argue from another. If our opponent believes nothing of divine revelation, there is no longer any means of proving the articles of faith by reasoning, but only of answering his objections—if he has any—against faith."

2

LUTHERAN WORLD FEDERATION (LWF)

Thus the question is raised and waits
for an answer, not today or tomorrow,
but it waits: Is the ecumenical movement
a church or is it not?[1]

—Dietrich Bonhoeffer

Background and Structure

Founded at its first assembly held in Lund, Sweden in 1947, the Lutheran World Federation (LWF) today consists of 140 member churches in 79 countries worldwide whose membership totals more than 70 million.[2] Taking its name from the magisterial branch of the sixteenth-century Protestant Reformation identified with Martin Luther (1483–1546), the LWF finds its doctrinal basis in its confession of "the Holy Scriptures of the Old and New Testaments to be the only source and norm of its doctrine, life and service. It sees in the three Ecumenical Creeds and in the Confessions of the Lutheran Church, especially in the unaltered Augsburg

Confession and the Small Catechism of Martin Luther, a pure exposition of the Word of God."[3]

The most authoritative structure within the LWF is the Assembly, which usually meets every six years. The most recent meeting was held in 2003 in Winnipeg, Canada, with the theme, "For the Healing of the World." The eleventh Assembly of the LWF, "Give Us Today Our Daily Bread," is to be held in Stuttgart, Germany in 2010. In addition to the Assembly, the LWF is governed by the Council consisting of fifty members (the president, treasurer, and 48 members elected by the Assembly). This Council "is responsible for the business of the Federation in the interim between ordinary Assemblies." Within the Council there is also an Executive Committee, consisting of various officers and chairpersons of program committees. This Executive Committee also serves as the Personnel Committee and the LWF Board of Trustees.[4] A third major structure within the LWF is the Secretariat, which is headed by a General Secretary appointed by the Council. The General Secretary "shall conduct the business of the Federation and carry out the decisions of the Assembly and the Council."[5] Whereas the President's responsibilities lie within the administration of the Assembly and the Council, the General Secretary is the basic administrative and bureaucratic authority within the Federation, as well as with contact and cooperation between other ecumenical groups, governmental bodies, and nongovernmental organizations.

The documents under examination here come out of the 2003 Assembly, and focus on neoliberal globalization. Official proceedings from the tenth Assembly were compiled and published following the meeting, along with background documents and commentary.[6] The texts under examination have been identified specifically as "Commitments the LWF has Made."[7] These texts, as affirmed by the Council and the Assembly, as well as authorized public declarations based on the approved document, "A Call to Participate in Transforming Economic Globalization," represent declarations from the highest levels of authority within the LWF.

A Call to Participate in Transforming Economic Globalization (2003)

A key aspect of the LWF's engagement with economic globalization is its opposition to the neoliberal paradigm, the predominant characteristic of the global situation in the post-Cold War era. It is in this context that "a new stage has been reached through Internet technologies and the dominance of the neoliberal paradigm."[8] A fundamental aspect of this neoliberal model is the contemporary phenomenon of economic globalization.

These two realities, namely neoliberal theory and economic globalization, are intimately linked. The LWF identifies some basic characteristics of this relationship, contending, "Driven by neoliberal theory, economic globalization places priority on the free movement of investment capital, profit maximization and growth, and the increasing reliance on market forces."[9] A message adopted by the 2003 Assembly describes the "false ideology" of neoliberal globalization as being "grounded on the assumption that the market, built on private property, unrestrained competition and the centrality of contracts, is the absolute law governing human life, society and the natural environment."[10] The LWF call goes on to delineate particular features of economic globalization, including:

> **Mobility across borders**: There has been an escalating movement of goods, services, capital (trade and investment), and speculative money across international borders.

> **Deregulation:** Regulations are dropped or liberalized in order to enable this movement to occur more freely.

31

Corporate power: A growing portion of the world's large economies are actually large corporations that are unaccountable to the public.

Privatization: Many public goods and services, such as water, electricity, health care, and education are being privatized.

Commodification of life: A monetary value is being placed on more and more areas of life, which can then be marketed worldwide.

Homogenization: While Western consumer-oriented ways of life are marketed around the world, local products and cultural practices are eventually disappearing.

Speculative investment: Buying and selling money instruments for the purpose of high short-term gain outpace trade in actual goods and services and long-term investment in production-oriented economic activity.

Loss of sovereignty: In the face of these trends, governments increasingly feel there is little they can do to protect their people and resources.[11]

The value judgments of these characterizations range from neutral (at best) to explicitly negative. Unlike many such ecumenical pronouncements, however, "A Call to Participate in Transforming Economic Globalization" does spare some recognition of potential benefits of globalization, however slight: "For some in our world, economic globalization brings economic growth and with it economic benefits. This has lifted people out of poverty and has created an abundance of goods and services, and even soaring standards of living for some."[12]

The basic problem, though, is that the few have benefited at the expense of the many. Immediately after noting that there have been some limited goods to result from economic globalization, the LWF call abruptly chastens any further potential optimism. Despite these limited economic benefits, the LWF call connects the economics of globalization with environmental degradation, noting that "on the whole the prevailing model of economic globalization is widening the gap between the wealthy and the rest of humanity at an alarming rate and threatening the earth's life-support systems." The LWF call goes on to soberly enumerate the implications: "The positive effects of globalization are far from being realized globally; globalization is **not** global in its benefits. Wealth and power are more concentrated than ever." To substantiate these claims, the LWF call summarizes the findings of a 2002 Social Watch Report showing that "over three billion people try to survive on less than 2 U.S. dollars a day, whereas the three richest persons have more than the GNP of the 48 poorest countries."[13]

Perhaps even more disturbing than these economic realities, however, are the corrosive cultural, social, and spiritual effects of globalization. Thus, claims the LWF, "What tends to be sacrificed through processes of economic globalization are spiritual values, cultural identity and diversity, and other aspects of life that cannot be measured in economic terms." Such realities "pose a central theological and moral challenge which the churches cannot ignore."[14] In acknowledging the priority of the spiritual corrosiveness of globalization, the LWF contends that the "the basic challenge" that must be faced is "the disempowerment or sense of hopelessness and helplessness that most people, churches and countries feel in the face of policies and practices related to economic globalization." This is in its most basic sense a "spiritual crisis" rather than merely a material or economic concern.[15]

It is on the basis of these claims that the LWF issues its call to transform economic globalization, using a variety of approaches. Some choose to prophetically denounce the current world order, others "seek to reform or redirect certain aspects of it," while others are intent on mitigating the deleterious effects of globalization as best they can.[16] For the LWF, the concept of transformation must embrace this spectrum of responses.

Another feature of the LWF call is its focus on the economic power of multinational corporations. This emphasis is explicitly defended against a corresponding emphasis on the authority and responsibility of governments. Indeed, it is a characteristic of neoliberal globalization that governments as well as peoples are marginalized by more powerful economic institutions: "In many places today, governments are experienced as the enemy or have lost much of their sovereign power, such that it is quite difficult to hold them accountable."[17] Instead of concerning itself with addressing governments who might be held responsible for their actions, the LWF call is especially focused on multinational corporations and tyrannical and corrupt governments.

In this way, the LWF call criticizes the undemocratic nature of such economic players, and this is a key aspect of the neoliberal critique:

> Today a growing portion of the world's large economies is unaccountable to the public as a whole. This is especially the case for transnational corporations and financial institutions. The current system of economic globalization limits the ability of people, governments and nations to insist on respect and negotiation of conditions when an outside company comes in to use their natural resources, infrastructure and their workforce. Poor and other vulnerable people must be able to participate with dignity in society, while being protected from arbitrary, unaccountable actions by governments, multinational corporations and other forces.[18]

The focus of this transformative engagement with neoliberal globalization is to realize the "primary purposes of economic life," identified as the responsibility "to sustain and promote the well-being of just and sustainable communities the world over," and "to serve the well-being of human beings and the rest of creation." This vision is contrasted with the situation imposed by neoliberal globalization, in which the purposes are "to maximize wealth or increase consumption by those who already have more than they need" and to have "human beings and the rest of creation being sacrificed for economic ends."[19]

Analysis

From the character of the LWF statements on economic globalization it is apparent that the organization views itself as having a responsibility to provide ethical leadership to the Lutheran churches, the broader ecumenical movement, and the world. In this sense, Bonhoeffer's question whether the ecumenical movement is a church or not continues to be answered in the affirmative. Identifying itself as "a communion of churches" the LWF sees in part that it "furthers worldwide among the member churches diaconic action, alleviation of human need, promotion of peace and human rights, social and economic justice, care for God's creation and sharing of resources."[20] In terms of its content, the LWF call continues to exhibit the characteristics of the *social action curia* identified by Ramsey, especially the "passion for numerous particular pronouncements on policy questions to the consequent neglect of basic decision- and action-oriented principles of ethical and political analysis."[21]

This summary examination of the LWF statements on economic life from the 2003 Assembly in Winnipeg bears out the concerns articulated by Ernest W. Lefever about the increasing influence of a neo-Marxist worldview on the ecumenical movement. The rubric of "neoliberal economic globalization" has become the watchword for ecumenical ethics. What Lefever calls "the neo-Marxist myth that colonialism, neocolonialism, and transnational corporations are the causes of poverty in the Third World" has been wholeheartedly embraced by the LWF statements.[22]

The ideological nature of these statements and conclusions are made manifest by the highly skewed description of the contemporary economic situation. Aside from brief mention of the limited benefits of liberalized global trade, benefits that are quickly passed over and marginalized, there is little in the way of balanced presentation of economic realities. Additionally, because ethical pronouncements immediately follow from whatever economic analysis is present, the moral guidance of the LWF statements is likewise skewed.

Moreover, there is nothing particularly novel or uniquely Christian about this critique of globalization. As the economists Victor Claar and Robin Klay note, "The streams of criticism and multiple motives of those who organize anti-globalization protests are difficult to disentangle."[23] In this area, the LWF and the broader ecumenical movement have simply joined a chorus of worldly voices decrying the evils of globalization. It is unclear what is accomplished by such denouncements beyond providing a thin veneer of religiosity to otherwise secular political activism.

Gaps Between Rich and Poor

A basic point of departure for the LWF critique of globalization is the claim that not all have benefited equally from increased liberalization of trade. Thus, the LWF call notes the "widening gap between the wealthy and the rest of humanity at an alarming rate," as if such a gap in and of itself were intrinsically and clearly morally dubious.[24] However, differences in income distribution can only be assumed to be unjust or unfair under a particular definition of justice as equal distribution or equal shares. There is another sense of justice, perhaps even a more basic sense, in which justice has to do with merit or desert.[25] On this view, it would be difficult to argue that unequal compensation is unjust if there is unequal performance, whether quantitative or qualitative. The emphasis of economic and ethical analysis should thus not be on the size of relative shares but rather on the overall prospects for prosperity—what philosopher David Schmidtz calls the improvement of "general life chances—on removing barriers to people bettering themselves not because barriers entrench inequality but simply because barriers are barriers."[26]

It is not clear then why the burden of proof ought to be on those who argue for the efficacy of globalization in increasing worldwide prosperity. As Claar and Klay note, "Globalization—that is, the increased movement of goods, money and people across national borders—is nothing other than an enlarged version of what happens in every town, state and country as markets expand and knit the component parts into a web of interdependence."[27] This sense of interdependence in which producers and consumers, buyers and sellers, each rely on the other to flourish is critical to understanding the moral potential of market economies, whether local or global in scale.

By contrast, the LWF perspective on globalization assumes that true human interrelation is only possible where the paradigm of economic globalization is rejected, amended, or transformed. Rather than neoliberal globalization, Christians are to attempt to realize a "globalization of solidarity," a reality "grounded in what it means to be a communion in which God in Christ sets us in relationship with one another."[28] While it is appropriate to acknowledge the qualitative difference in fellowship experienced among Christians and among human beings in merely civil affairs, completely overlooked in the LWF account is the fundamental relationship of interdependence that is at the core of all market economies.

Using an analogy of interstate commerce between Montana and California and applying it to the international scene, Claar and Klay demonstrate the importance of global trade to those in developing nations. "Third World countries, just like Montana," they observe, "stand to gain from strong sales of their products. The observation that Americans consume more than Chinese …, for example, has no more significance than a similar observation that Californians earn and consume more than Montanans."[29] That is, the moral status of some level of consumption is not obviously dubious when in a system of global trade those in developing nations depend for their profits on demand from those in other nations. Indeed, it is not only those in the First World who consume goods. As Claar and Klay note, "Third World people sell their products—like textiles, tropical foodstuffs and electronic goods—in international markets because, by selling their relatively abundant and low-cost products, they can buy relatively abundant and low-cost goods from trading partners."[30]

Pointing to a book by Indian economist Surjit S. Bhalla (available at the time the LWF's call was issued in 2003), Claar and Klay rightly note that in general and on the global scale, there is "stunning evidence of shrinking income gaps between First and Third World peoples, along with closing gaps in literacy, infant mortality, life expectancy, educational achievement and political and civic liberties."[31] Of course, this progress is not uniform, and Claar and Klay point out some of the multitudes of factors that either promote or retard economic growth, including accidents of geography, bad government and public policies, and excessive government regulation.[32] Sometimes, as Schmidtz observes, barriers are barriers.[33] Some can be removed or leveled; others cannot.

Accountability and Multinational Corporations

The main institutional targets of the LWF critique of globalization are multinational corporations (MNCs), and the basic thrust of the complaint is that these institutions are not publicly accountable.[34] It is true that corporations of whatever size are not typically accountable in the same way that democratically elected governments are, but this is no reason to presume that this is unjust or inappropriate. Businesses and governments, just like the family and the church, are distinct institutions and ought to be directed according to the principles proper to each.

There are at least two ways in which most multinational corporations are accountable to the public, at least in some sense. First, for many multinationals that are publicly traded, there are stringent rules and regulations in place for disclosure of financial information, payout of dividends, and corporate governance. A publicly traded multinational corporation is accountable in one way or another to its stockholding public. Accountability in this sense does not come free, but it is freely available to those who wish to purchase a share.

Second, all corporations and businesses, of any size or composition, are accountable to their clients and customers. To pursue the line of analogy between governments and corporations, each purchase on the part of a customer is a kind of vote of affirmation for the producer. In a free economy, consumers are at liberty to use whatever criteria for purchase they desire. Many will simply choose the most inexpensive option. Others are free to buy with a particular agenda, whether aesthetic, political, social, or moral. The corporate profit motive guarantees that companies can never simply ignore consumer demands. Thus, writes moral philosopher Samuel Gregg, "If the goal in the market is to obtain wealth, profit through trade is a powerful motivation to provide consumers what consumers demand at efficient costs to the company."[35] In the case of multinationals, the accountability complaint holds no greater credence because "MNCs do not continue in business unless they offer valuable services and products at attractive prices to their suppliers and customers."[36] Simple characterization of multinational corporations as threats to sovereign nations underscores the ideological nature of the LWF critique and undermines its credibility on aspects that do warrant closer consideration. A credible critique, however, can only exist on the basis of fair-minded analysis, and the unbalanced characterization of multinational corporations in the LWF call does not approach this level.

As Claar and Klay observe, those corporations that rise to multinational status are those that are the best at what businesses do. "Starting with success in their home market, the most productive firms ultimately extend their reach beyond political boundaries because they are able to offer higher prices to sellers of their inputs and lower prices to consumers of their products than could businesses confined to one state or country."[37] In this sense, then, the critics of globalization are right to target multinational corporations, because without these institutions large-scale international trade would be nearly impossible.

For this reason Claar and Klay wonder at the virulence of the critics of antiglobalization leveled against MNCs, and offer a possible explanation:

> Perhaps it is because the critics do not understand the key roles MNCs play in getting Third World products to world markets, supplying inputs to Third World farmers and businesses, and financing Third World production. When they are able to sell machinery, consumer goods, and certain foodstuffs (e.g., the wheat needed to bake bread) at prices that could not be matched by local producers, MNCs are helping Third World people.[38]

The inability of the LWF critique to distinguish between the potential threats represented by corporate economic power (gained by voluntary exchange) and governmental coercive power (gained by police or military force) contributes to ignorance of the good the multinational corporations do. Claar and Klay call this a kind of "selective blindness" that

often "prevents us from appreciating how criticisms of globalization may undermine the very forces that are vital to
progress against poverty."[39] This blindness also contributes
to ignorance of the aspects of globalization that warrant the
most critical discernment.

A valid point of concern with regard to multinational corporations is not that they are by nature unaccountable to the
public but lies instead in their potential to corrupt and pervert
the coercive power of the state. There is perhaps no more
obvious example than in the corporate lobby for governmental subsidy. It is true, as Claar and Klay observe, that when
MNCs provide lower cost foodstuffs than would otherwise
be available to local producers they are "helping Third World
people."[40] It is also true that when MNCs are only able to do
so because they are the recipients of the largesse of developed
nations in the form of subsidies, they undermine the ability of
food producers in the developing world to compete and thrive.
This kind of corruption of the economic sphere through the
cooption of governmental coercive force hinders rather than
helps those in the Third World.[41] The LWF concern ought not
to be with the economic power of multinational corporations
as such but rather with the wedding of corporate power to
the coercive power of the government.

Spiritual Hopelessness and Material Helplessness

More central to the LWF call to transform economic globalization than these kinds of specifically economic concerns,
however, are particularly moral and spiritual judgments about
the effects of globalization. The existential sense of disempowerment or hopelessness follows logically from the assumptions
about the impunity with which multinational corporations
operate. This, then, is the ecumenical movement's basic challenge as identified by the LWF, to engage "the disempowerment or sense of hopelessness and helplessness that most

people, churches and countries feel in the face of policies and practices related to economic globalization."[42] The reasoning is simple. If the center of power lies with multinational corporations and these corporations are by definition unaccountable, there is little hope for substantial transformation of globalization.

This line of reasoning is entirely dependent, however, on the veracity of the underlying economic analysis. If economic globalization is not in the first place predatory or deleterious but rather mutually beneficial and empowering, the basis for the spiritual diagnosis of hopelessness and helplessness disappears. Theologian John Schneider has written extensively on the challenge of properly valuing the gift of wealth and the material blessings of God. On Schneider's account, the appropriate response to the affluence created by the modern market economy is one of delight and celebration of God's gifts, rather than of despair or hopelessness.[43] Schneider writes, "There is a spiritual connection, after all, between dignified work—the creation and realization of one's vision—and reaping the fruits of that work in relative security and freedom."[44]

There is of course no guarantee that affluence leads to either temporal or spiritual happiness. The human ability to properly value material goods is directly related to the person's spiritual state. Only where God is rightly valued above all else can other goods be properly and relatively valued. As Schneider rightly observes, "People who lack spiritual resources and are miserable to begin with often become even more miserable amid their possessions. Increased wealth merely gives them more ways to be unhappy. Even people who are not miserable to begin with may become spoiled and lost in mindless, obsessive consumption."[45] It is in this way true that there are spiritual dangers associated with the increase of wealth. As Bonhoeffer notes, "It is hard for the well-fed and the powerful to comprehend God's judgment and God's grace."[46] Those who are wealthy often become spiritually slothful, assuming that their apparent material self-sufficiency gives evidence of their spiritual self-sufficiency. For those who are poor, the spiritual dangers may well be envy or despair.

Even so, the critique of economic globalization contains within it an implicit affirmation of the basic good of affluence. Schneider wonders of these critics: "Do Western thinkers truly mean to imply that the poor are really better off in conditions of non-affluence? For those seeking liberation from poverty for themselves and for their people, that indeed seems a strange and self-defeating premise to adopt."[47] In truth, rather than adopting a posture of spiritual hopelessness or material helplessness, the disruption of the antiglobalization logic on the basis of progress against global poverty warrants cautious and circumspect optimism. Thus, Claar and Klay write, "The trajectory of sustained improvement in many parts of the Third World … is a powerful reason for hope."[48]

Albeit, they add that this is to be a "reasoned hope," a hope that does not embrace "calls for revolutionary changes based on misguided messianic expectations." A major component of neo-Marxist ideology is its emphasis on the perfectability of social, economic, and political improvement. This runs counter to a Christian perspective that recognizes the depths of the fall into sin and the ongoing corruption of human beings. Christians are called to be obedient, not necessarily to be successful. Christians might well be successful in improving economic conditions for many throughout the world, and Claar and Klay are right to emphasize the need to be "thinking in the long run"—a perspective that lends itself to celebration in the final consummation represented in Christ's return.[49]

Indeed, Lefever consistently invokes the theological assessment appearing in the report of the 1948 Amsterdam Assembly, "The Church and the Disorder of Society." Speaking of the kind of despair expressed in the LWF statement, the Amsterdam report contends, "The Christian faith leaves no room for such despair, being based on the fact that the

Kingdom of God is firmly established in Christ and will come by God's act despite all human failure."[50] It is in this context that Bonhoeffer wonders:

> Who actually says that all worldly problems should and can be solved? Perhaps to God the unsolved condition of these problems may be more important than their solution, namely, as a pointer to the human fall and to God's redemption. Human problems are perhaps so entangled, so wrongly posed, that they are in fact really impossible to solve. (The problem of poor and rich can never be solved in any other way than leaving it unsolved.)[51]

This is, as Bonhoeffer also observes, no excuse for idleness or disobedience, but it does illustrate the reality that as long as there is sin in the world, there will be poverty, hunger, disease, violence, and death.

Providence and Self-Interest

The LWF call explicitly cites a 2002 Social Watch Report to substantiate claims about the increasing gap between rich and poor and the consolidation of economic power in the hands of a few. In the prologue to this report, Roberto Bissio writes, "Wealth and power is more concentrated now than ever before. Joseph Stiglitz, awarded the Nobel Prize for Economy 2001, concluded: '[W]e do not see Adam Smith's 'invisible hand,' because it doesn't exist.' For the market to operate as an efficient distribution mechanism all participants should concur to it with the same information, something that never happens in practice."[52] If this is the basic frame of reference for LWF ethical and economic analysis, there is little wonder that a sense of hopelessness and helplessness pervades.

There is, however, a more fundamental reason for hope than the tangible results of economic analysis. Rather than holding a view that "assumes equal partners with equal access to information, technical expertise and trade conditions, but that is a far cry from the harsh disparities in the real world," as the LWF characterization of neoliberal theory states, there is a firm basis in the Christian doctrine of general providence to find hope that economic relations can and do reflect some form of justice.[53] Indeed, as the economists Robin Klay and John Lunn have written, the Christian doctrine of general providence has secular corollaries in economic doctrines such as Adam Smith's invisible hand and Friedrich Hayek's concept of spontaneous order.[54] Claar and Klay similarly contend that "although human beings may use markets to pursue evil, as well as good, we do not doubt that, under God's providential care, markets coordinate billions of free decisions that ultimately bless many."[55] This sense of providential administration of the economy does not depend on any finite human knowledge or access to information, but rather on the omniscience and benevolence of God.

Neither does this providential administration depend on humans' acting only virtuously. As Klay and Lunn soberly observe, "Not all people are Christians and not all Christians behave selflessly all of the time."[56] It is a measure of divine grace that the self-interested actions of many do not always or inevitably have negative social effects. Indeed, within a market economy, even the vice of selfishness (or immoderate self-interest) can paradoxically result in benefits to the larger society. God has so ordered the economy that he is able to bring material blessings through fallen and corrupted human action. This reality does nothing to mitigate the spiritual consequences of such sin, but it does prod Christians to recognize the general or common gifts of divine providence.

In this way, those who recognize the benefits of economic globalization do not need to defend some utopian or idealistic model that has no correlate in the real world nor do they need to work for the perfection of any world system. As Gregg writes, we should not "presume that sound economics is the universal elixir for all the problems that plague the social order."[57] The global market system is neither perfect nor incorruptible. It has its flaws just as does any reality in this fallen world. Recognition of these flaws should not prevent affirmation of its beneficial features.

The LWF position on globalization, however, prevents it from achieving a balanced perspective that allows it to account for the positive gifts provided by God in the production of wealth. This economic failing, in line with Lefever's critique, is exacerbated by the LWF's insistence on making specific political and economic declarations. This level of specificity and particularity runs afoul of Ramsey's criticism, that the church should be much more circumspect and chastened in its social witness. These two faults combine to raise the question whether the LWF and abuse of its platform amount to a failure to function as an institutional form of the church. This would place the LWF in the position of being a social action committee made up of Christians, as Bonhoeffer notes, rather than an expression of the church as an institution.

Notes

1. Dietrich Bonhoeffer, "The Confessing Church and the Ecumenical Movement," in *No Rusty Swords: Letters, Lectures and Notes 1928–1936*, trans. Edwin H. Robertson and John Bowden, ed. Edwin H. Robertson (New York: Harper & Row, 1965) 334–35.

2. See Jens Holger Schjørring, Prasanna Kumari, and Norman A. Hjelm, eds., *From Federation to Communion: The History of the Lutheran World Federation* (Minneapolis: Fortress Press, 1997). For background of the Lutheran World Federation and its predecessors, see E. Clifford Nelson, *The Rise of World Lutheranism: An American Perspective* (Philadelphia: Fortress Press, 1982).

3. *Constitution of the Lutheran World Federation* (as adopted by the LWF Eighth Assembly, Curitiba, Brazil, 1990, includ-

ing amendments adopted by the LWF Ninth Assembly, Hong Kong, 1997), art. II. On the ecumenical implications of the Augsburg Confession, see Heiko A. Oberman, "From Protest to Confession: The *Confessio Augustana* as a Critical Test of True Ecumenism," in *The Reformation: Roots and Ramifications*, trans. Andrew Colin Gow (New York: T&T Clark, 2004).

4. *Constitution of the Lutheran World Federation*, art. VIII.

5. *Constitution of the Lutheran World Federation*, art. XII.

6. Lutheran World Federation, *Communion, Responsibility, Accountability: Responding as a Lutheran Communion to Neoliberal Globalization*, ed. Karen L. Bloomquist (Geneva: Lutheran World Federation, 2004).

7. "A Call to Participate in Transforming Economic Globalization," in *Communion, Responsibility, Accountability*, 113–24; and "'For the Healing of the World,' Excerpts from the 2003 LWF Assembly Message," in *Communion, Responsibility, Accountability*, 125–30.

8. "A Call to Participate in Transforming Economic Globalization," 114.

9. "A Call to Participate in Transforming Economic Globalization," 114. Elsewhere an explicit example of "neoliberal economic policies" is identified with the "Washington Consensus." See "For the Healing of the World," 125.

10. "For the Healing of the World," 125.

11. "A Call to Participate in Transforming Economic Globalization," 114. Elsewhere the litany of indictments against globalization are said to include: (1) a growing gap between rich and poor, (2) the marginalization of indigenous peoples, (3) domination of weaker nations by means of international debt, (4) denial of access to the globalization of information, (5) shrinking resources available to churches, (6) increased unemployment, (7) barriers to migration, and (8) powerlessness and unwillingness on the part of governments to protect their citizens. See "For the Healing of the World," 125–26.

12. "A Call to Participate in Transforming Economic Globalization," 115.

13. "A Call to Participate in Transforming Economic Globalization," 115. See also "The Social Impact of Globalisation in the World," *Social Watch Report*, no. 6 (2002).

14. "A Call to Participate in Transforming Economic Globalization," 115.

15. "A Call to Participate in Transforming Economic Globalization," 116. Yet, even so, the economic realities have a clear impact on spiritual identity. See "A Call to Participate in Transforming Economic Globalization," 120: "Economic globalization tends to weaken those very bonds that theologically are constitutive of who we are in relation to others. Vast inequities are troubling because of this relational nature of human life. This understanding transforms radical individualism into community with others, ruthless competition into cooperation with others. Production that uses others is transformed into participation in the life of others."

16. "A Call to Participate in Transforming Economic Globalization," 115.

17. "A Call to Participate in Transforming Economic Globalization," 119.

18. "A Call to Participate in Transforming Economic Globalization," 123.

19. "A Call to Participate in Transforming Economic Globalization," 121.

20. *Constitution of the Lutheran World Federation*, art. III.

21. Paul Ramsey, *Who Speaks for the Church? A Critique of the 1966 Geneva Conference on Church and Society* (Nashville: Abingdon Press, 1967), 13.

22. Ernest W. Lefever, *Amsterdam to Nairobi: The World Council of Churches and the Third World* (Washington, D.C.: Ethics and Public Policy Center, 1979), 52.

23. Victor V. Claar and Robin J. Klay, *Economics in Christian Perspective: Theory, Policy and Life Choices* (Downers Grove: Inter-Varsity Press, IVP Academic, 2007), 143.

24. "A Call to Participate in Transforming Economic Globalization," 115.

25. For a good survey from a secular and philosophical perspective of the variegated landscape inhabited by the term *justice*, see David Schmidtz, *Elements of Justice* (New York: Cambridge University Press, 2006).

26. Schmidtz, *Elements of Justice*, 118–19.

27. Claar and Klay, *Economics in Christian Perspective*, 144.

28. "A Call to Participate in Transforming Economic Globalization," 118.

29. Claar and Klay, *Economics in Christian Perspective*, 146–47.

30. Claar and Klay, *Economics in Christian Perspective*, 151.

31. Claar and Klay, *Economics in Christian Perspective*, 157. See Surjit S. Bhalla, *Imagine There's No Country: Poverty, Inequality, and Growth in an Era of Globalization* (Washington, D.C.: Institute for International Economics, 2002). See also Jagdish N. Bhagwati, *In Defense of Globalization* (New York: Oxford University Press, 2004).

32. Claar and Klay, *Economics in Christian Perspective*, 155–56.

33. Schmidtz, *Elements of Justice*, 118–19.

34. "A Call to Participate in Transforming Economic Globalization," 123: "Today a growing portion of the world's large economies is unaccountable to the public as a whole. This is especially the case for transnational corporations and financial institutions."

35. Samuel J. Gregg, *Economic Thinking for the Theologically Minded* (Lanham: University Press of America, 2001), 127.

36. Claar and Klay, *Economics in Christian Perspective*, 150.

37. Claar and Klay, *Economics in Christian Perspective*, 150.

38. Claar and Klay, *Economics in Christian Perspective*, 150–51.

39. Claar and Klay, *Economics in Christian Perspective*, 152.

40. Claar and Klay, *Economics in Christian Perspective*, 151.

41. The vast and complex network of agricultural subsidies in the United States is an example of this.

42. "A Call to Participate in Transforming Economic Globalization," 116.

43. See John Schneider, *The Good of Affluence: Seeking God in a Culture of Wealth* (Grand Rapids: Eerdmans, 2002).

44. Schneider, *The Good of Affluence*, 37.

45. Schneider, *The Good of Affluence*, 39. Consider here the biblical example of Solomon.

46. Dietrich Bonhoeffer, *Ethics*, trans. Reinhard Krauss, Charles C. West, Douglas W. Scott, ed. Clifford J. Green, Dietrich Bonhoeffer Works 6 (Minneapolis: Fortress Press, 2005), 162.

47. Schneider, *The Good of Affluence*, 40.

48. Claar and Klay, *Economics in Christian Perspective*, 157.

49. Claar and Klay, *Economics in Christian Perspective*, 160.

50. "The Church and the Disorder of Society," a report from the Amsterdam Assembly of the World Council of Churches (Geneva: World Council of Churches, 1948). Quoted in Lefever, *Nairobi to Vancouver*, 7. The eschatological perspective of these competing opinions is an area that has important consequences and warrants further exploration. In this vein, see Calvin P. Van Reken, "Christians in This World: Pilgrims or Settlers?" *Calvin Theological Journal* 43, no. 2 (November 2008): 234–56; and H. Richard Niebuhr, "The Kingdom of God and Eschatology in the Social Gospel and in Barthianism," in *Theology, History, and Culture: Major Unpublished Writings*, ed. William Stacy Johnson (New Haven: Yale University Press, 1996), 117–23.

51. Bonhoeffer, *Ethics*, 354–55.

52. Social Watch, "The Social Impact of Globalisation in the World," *Social Watch Report*, no. 6 (2002): 9–10.

53. "A Call to Participate in Transforming Economic Globalization," 115.

54. Robin Klay and John Lunn, "The Relationship of God's Providence to Market Economies and Economic Theory," *Journal of Markets & Morality* 6, no. 2 (Fall 2003): 541–64. See also the four-part controversy between Michael T. Dempsey and Klay and Lunn, "What Bearing, If Any, Does the Christian Doctrine of Providence Have Upon the Operation of the Market Economy," *Journal of Markets & Morality* 8, no. 2 (Fall 2005): 481–519.

55. Claar and Klay, *Economics in Christian Perspective*, 48.

56. Klay and Lunn, "The Relationship of God's Providence to Market Economies and Economic Theory," 558.

57. Gregg, *Economic Thinking for the Theologically Minded*, 47.

3

WORLD COMMUNION
OF REFORMED
CHURCHES (WCRC)

*Can it really be believed that a popery of the
expert, whose particular voice shortly becomes
the church's recommendation, no matter how
expert he is, would be the way to improve the
present popery of committees and conferences?*[1]

—Paul Ramsey

Background and Structure

The World Communion of Reformed Churches (WCRC) is
the result of a merger between two previous Reformed ecumenical groups, the World Alliance of Reformed Churches
(WARC) and the Reformed Ecumenical Council (REC),
scheduled to occur during a Uniting General Council held
in Grand Rapids, Michigan, USA, in June 2010. The previous year, the executive committees circulated a proposed
constitution for the WCRC, in which it is stated, "The World
Communion of Reformed Churches succeeds the Reformed
Ecumenical Council and the World Alliance of Reformed

Churches and its antecedents, as a united ecumenical body for Reformed churches."[2] The new organization consists of 227 member churches in 108 countries, whose membership exceeds 80 million. The doctrinal basis of the WCRC lies in its commitment "to embody a Reformed identity as articulated in the historic Reformed confessions and the Ecumenical Creeds of the early church, and as continued in the life and witness of the Reformed community."[3]

The general council is the highest authoritative body within the WCRC, and is scheduled to meet every seven years.[4] The executive committee meets annually and conducts business for the WCRC between meetings of the general council. In addition, the executive committee is responsible for authorizing "the President and/or the General Secretary to speak for the World Communion of Reformed Churches between meetings of the General Council."[5] The president is thus elected by the general council but empowered to speak as an institutional representative by the executive committee.[6] The general secretary serves as the "chief executive officer" of the WCRC and is "responsible to the General Council and to the Executive Committee to direct and coordinate the work of the World Communion of Reformed Churches."[7] An added layer of leadership exists in the form of executive secretaries, whose number and authority are "determined by the Executive Committee upon recommendation of the General Secretary."[8] The constitution further lays out the procedure for the formation of committees and commissions (answerable directly to the general council and executive committee) as well as of offices and departments (answerable indirectly to the general council and executive committee as mediated by the general secretary) and regional councils, "accountable to the General Council of the World Communion of Reformed Churches through its appointed administrative structures."[9]

The document under examination here is *The Accra Confession: Covenanting for Justice and the Earth*, which was adopted by the World Alliance of Reformed Churches (WARC) at its twenty-fourth general council held in Accra, Ghana, in 2004.[10] At the time, this was the highest possible endorsement of the document by the larger of the two organizations that form the WCRC. In addition, WARC has taken steps to bring the Accra Confession into the newly formed WCRC, in part by sponsoring an ongoing series of publications and events focused on the confession, including a "Global Dialogue on the Accra Confession," held in Johannesburg, South Africa, in September 2009.[11] Moreover, the Accra Confession represents the fruit of a broader commitment with the ecumenical movement, including the World Council of Churches, to build a "covenanting for justice" movement.

The Accra Confession: Covenanting for Justice and the Earth (2004)

The Accra Confession places itself within the context of ongoing ecumenical discussions about the theological and moral status of questions related to "economic injustice and ecological destruction," pointing specifically to the call of the South African delegation at a consultation in Kitwe in 1995, in which it was reported: "It is our painful conclusion that the African reality of poverty caused by an unjust economic world order has gone beyond an ethical problem and become a theological one. It now constitutes a *status confessionis*. The gospel to the poor is at stake in the very mechanism of the global economy today" (art. 1).[12] At the twenty-third general council of the World Alliance of Reformed Churches held at Debrecen, Hungary, in 1997, the council decided "to enter into a process of 'recognition, education, and confession (*processus confessionis*)'" concerning the realities of economic globalization (art. 1). Citing the "ongoing realities of human trafficking and the oppression of the global economic system," the twenty-fourth general council decided in the form of the Accra Confession "to take a decision of faith commitment" (arts. 3, 4).

After the introductory articles, the first major section of the Accra Confession focuses on "reading the signs of the times" in the form of examining economic and environmental statistics. These statistics witness to the "product of an unjust economic system defended and protected by political and military might" (art. 6). Among the most egregious economic consequences of this global economic system are (1) increasing concentration of wealth in the hands of few, (2) corresponding poverty resulting in widespread death, (3) increasing burden of debt among poor nations, (4) the pursuit of "resource-driven wars," and (5) death as the result of preventable diseases (art. 7). The effects of "unlimited growth among industrialized countries and the drive for profit of transnational corporations" also include serious environmental consequences, including: (1) species and habitat loss, (2) climate change, (3) "high levels of radioactivity," and (4) the creation and patenting of genetically modified organisms (art. 8).

Tracing the origins of these troubling realities, the Accra Confession identifies these effects as "directly related to the development of neoliberal economic globalization." The confession goes on to define four basic tenets of neoliberal economic globalization:

- unrestrained competition, consumerism, and the unlimited economic growth and accumulation of wealth is the best for the whole world;

- the ownership of private property has no social obligation;

- capital speculation, liberalization and deregulation of the market, privatization of public utilities and national resources, unrestricted access for foreign investments and imports, lower taxes, and the unrestricted movement of capital will achieve wealth for all;

- social obligations, protection of the poor and the weak, trade unions, and relationships between people, are subordinate to the processes of economic growth and capital accumulation (art. 9).

The confession sums up neoliberal economic globalization as "an ideology that claims to be without alternative, demanding an endless flow of sacrifices from the poor and creation. It makes the false promise that it can save the world through the creation of wealth and prosperity, claiming sovereignty over life and demanding total allegiance, which amounts to idolatry" (art. 10).

Despite the severity of the situation as summarily depicted in the previous sections, the Accra Confession claims to "recognize the enormity and complexity of the situation" and testifies to "not seek simple answers." The complexity of the economic situation is essentially the result of the combination of transnational interests. The confession identifies this as the neoliberal "empire," or, "the coming together of economic, cultural, political and military power that constitutes a system of domination led by powerful nations to protect and defend their own interests" (art. 11).

The conclusion of the section devoted to prophetic discernment traces the recent history of neoliberal economic theory, in which "the transnationalization of capital, neoliberalism has set out to dismantle the welfare functions of the state." The welfare state represents a direct threat to neoliberal economic theory, since according to neoliberalism "the purpose of the economy is to increase profits and return for the owners of production and financial capital, while excluding the majority of the people and treating nature as a commodity" (art. 12). The distinction between classical liberal economics and neoliberal economics is essentially that the latter has been elevated to a transnational scale and has taken the form of economic globalization.

This has led to a corresponding globalization of the "political and legal institutions" that protect global markets, especially including the "government of the United States of America and its allies, together with international finance and trade institutions (International Monetary Fund [IMF], World Bank, World Trade Organization)." These structures "use political, economic, or military alliances to protect and advance the interest of capital owners" (art. 13). Throughout all this, the Accra Confession discerns "the dramatic convergence of the economic crisis with the integration of economic globalization and geopolitics backed by neoliberal ideology" (art. 14).

In response to these realities, the Accra Confession identifies itself as a confession, "not meaning a classical doctrinal confession, because the World Alliance of Reformed Churches cannot make such a confession, but to show the necessity and urgency of an active response to the challenges of our time and the call of Debrecen" (art. 15). The confession amounts to a message to the member churches, an occasion and invitation for them to reflect on the "common witness" represented in the document. Even though the Accra Confession cannot be understood as "a classical doctrinal confession," it does identify itself as addressing a situation in which the confession either for or against Christ and his church must be made. Thus, the Accra Confession reflects a *status confessionis*, a situation in which such a confession is called for, as "the integrity of our faith is at stake if we remain silent or refuse to act in the face of the current system of neoliberal economic globalization" (art. 16).

This explicitly confessional component of the document outlines a series of propositions ("We believe …") with corresponding denouncements ("Therefore we reject …"). For instance, on the basis of the belief that "God is sovereign over all creation" (art. 18), the Accra Confession rejects "the current world economic order imposed by global neoliberal capitalism and any other economic system, including absolute planned economies, which defy God's covenant by excluding the poor, the vulnerable and the whole of creation from the fullness of life" (art. 19). Because "God has made a covenant with all of creation" (art. 20) in the form of his covenant with Noah (Gen. 9:18–12), the confession denounces "the culture of rampant consumerism and the competitive greed and self-ishness of the neoliberal economic global market system, or any other system which claims there is no alternative" (art. 21). Given that "any economy of the household of life, given to us by God's covenant to sustain life, is accountable to God" (art. 22), the document rejects "the unregulated accumulation of wealth and limitless growth that has already cost the lives of millions and destroyed much of God's creation" (art. 23).

In this way, the confession also denounces priority of "prof-its before people," as well as the privatization of "those gifts of God meant for all," rejecting "any teaching which justifies those who support, or fail to resist, such an ideology in the name of the gospel" (art. 25). Similarly denounced are the-ologies and doctrines that privilege the rich over the poor or that teach that human beings and their interests "dominate nature," (art. 27), or "any church practice or teaching which excludes the poor and care for creation, in its mission" (art. 29). Finally, given the call to form visible unity out of the church's diversity, the Accra Confession decries "any attempt in the life of the church to separate justice and unity" (art. 31). This section of confession concludes with a confession of sin and repentance (art. 34) as well as a statement of recognition that civil disobedience is sometimes necessary (art. 35).

The final section of the document outlines the practical responses that should be taken in light of what has been con-fessed. In particular, the confession urges member churches to continue the process of engagement with the confession in various ways. For those churches that have not yet recognized the confession in any formal way, the call is to "deepen their education and move forward towards confession" (art. 38). For those churches that have accepted the confession, it must be taught at the level of the local congregation (art. 39). To this end, the General Council specifically endorses the Public Issues Committee's recommendations on economic and ecological justice (art. 40) as well as the ongoing cooperation with other like-minded initiatives, both within the ecumenical movement and without, including interfaith as well as secular and populist movements (art. 41).

Analysis

The Accra Confession is explicitly intended to be an official form of witness on the part of the Christian church, at least insofar as represented by the World Alliance of Reformed Churches. To Bonhoeffer's ecclesiastical critical question to the ecumenical movement, the Accra Confession answers vociferously in the affirmative. Indeed, the Accra Confession and its supporting documents explicitly note the church struggle in Germany of the 1930s, and the Barmen Declaration (1934), as relevant antecedents for the aims of the Accra document.[13] The Accra Confession distinguishes itself from the "classic doctrinal confessions" of the Reformed churches of the sixteenth and seventeenth centuries, however, as intended more "to show the necessity and urgency of an active response to the challenges of our time and the call of Debrecen" (art. 15), given the ecclesiastical limits of the authority given to WARC. Even so, the Accra Confession does not merely call for "active response" but also explicitly draws lines of orthodoxy and orthopraxis between those who affirm the specific positions articulated by the confession and those who do not.

It is on this level of particularity that the Accra Confession is liable to the ethical critique raised by Paul Ramsey, namely, that it makes specific policy judgments rather than being satisfied with articulating the general principles that should be applied in the context of concrete circumstances. Thus, the Accra Confession denounces specific policies such as privatization (art. 25) and the patenting of genetically modified organisms (art. 8), as well as specific governments and institutions, such as the United States and the IMF (art. 13).

With respect to Lefever's economic critique of the ecumenical movement, the Accra Confession displays all the characteristics of a position defined in terms of a specific ideological complaint. That is, the economic positions and viewpoints expressed in the Accra Confession are materially consistent with the neo-Marxist liberation position criticized by Lefever as well as that previously found in the statements of the Lutheran World Federation.

Neo-Marxist Ideology

The South African economist Stan du Plessis has recently written a thorough critique of the economic perspective articulated in the Accra Confession that bears closer attention.[14] Du Plessis, observing the ideological edge present in the Accra statement, writes, "the Accra Declaration reads the 'signs of the times' through narrowly ideological lenses." The consequence of this ideological perspective is that "the 'Confession of Faith' rejects a series of claims about the economy that no one would defend in the positive. This ideological approach is not promising, as it substitutes a narrow ideology for a critical understanding of modern economies."[15] The Accra Confession claims to not be looking for simple (or simplistic) explanations of the current maladies facing the world (art. 11). Even so, the document boils down the complexity of world political and economic life to a single destructive cause: neoliberalism.

Indeed, the complexity present in the Accra Confession's perspective does not flow from an appreciation of the variety of players involved, from individual consumers, workers, and businesspersons to multinational corporations and non-governmental organizations and everything in between but rather from the recognition that the neoliberal order *itself* is complex. The answer for where blame ought to be assigned as expressed in the document is, in point of fact, quite simple. The world's economic "crisis is directly related to the development of neoliberal economic globalization" (art. 9).

As du Plessis aptly notes, however, such a simplistic explanation ought to be approached with skepticism. Thus, he writes with regard to neoliberalism: "It is not at all clear that a coherent ideology by that name exists, and when it appears, it does so almost exclusively on the pages of those who proceed to reject it."[16] We are left with a neoliberal ideology that has no exemplar in the sense that anyone has expressed a positive platform or program.[17] As du Plessis observes: "While unable to define neoliberalism in a conceptually coherent manner, the critical literature moved in a different direction to construct a historical narrative that serves to demonstrate the nature and influence of neoliberalism."[18] Du Plessis goes on to detail this narrative, which is manifest in brief outline in articles 12 and 13 of the Accra Confession, and judges it to be unconvincing: "the suspect ideology [i.e., neoliberalism] exists mainly (or even exclusively) in the minds of its opponents."[19]

Du Plessis finds a final shortfall of the Accra Confession's approach in that "it substitutes a narrow ideology for a critical understanding of modern economies, the kind of understanding that Christians need to make this imperfect world a little less so every year."[20] That is, the kind of tone and perspective adopted by the document "precludes participation" in reasoned policy debate.[21] Du Plessis goes on to masterfully illustrate this fault in the case of the confession's description of the purpose of the market economy (art. 13) and the distribution of wealth (arts. 7, 12). The point of du Plessis' critique, which is shared by this present larger engagement with the ecumenical movement, is "to demonstrate that we should not be so easily satisfied by narrowly ideological accounts of systems as complex as the economy" and to embrace an approach that "opens space for listening, for real debate and for persuasion."[22]

Ecumenical Confession

Part of the endemic shortcoming of the Accra Confession that contributes to all of the problems enumerated by du Plessis is the document's malformed approach to what contemporary confession ought to be. Apart from the specifics of whether this or that economic fact is correct or not, the Accra Confession fails to appreciate and protect space for vigorous and genuine discourse on prudential matters. Bonhoeffer's concern about the ecclesiastical status of the church applies precisely at this point because he understood that an affirmative answer meant that there were certain limits to what the institutional church ought to say and do. This care, this circumspection, is what Bonhoeffer means when he refers to the "moderate and pastoral bounds" of the task given to the spokespersons of the ecumenical movement.[23] It is where the ecumenical movement moves beyond these moderate bounds that its status as church comes into question, and this is how Ramsey's critique immediately raises Bonhoeffer's question.

Where the church ceases to speak and act as the church is supposed to, the question must immediately follow whether or not it is still the church. For Bonhoeffer, this can only be answered affirmatively when the church has fully embraced its responsibility to confess itself to be for its Lord and against his enemies. This is what Bonhoeffer describes as the "living confession." Thus, writes Bonhoeffer: "There can only be a church as a Confessing Church, i.e., as a church which confesses to be for its Lord and against his enemies. A church without a confession or free from one is not a church, but a sect, and makes itself master of the Bible and the Word of God."

Bonhoeffer goes on to define a confession as "the church's formulated answer to the Word of God in Holy Scripture, expressed in its own words."[24]

In addition, Bonhoeffer defines this living confession to be "a confession in which it is really a matter of life or death. A naturally formulated, clear, theologically based, true confession."[25] It is this standard-of-living confession, however, that the Accra Confession fails to achieve. It is true, as the Accra Confession claims, that "economic systems are a matter of life or death" (art. 6), but this is not the case in such a way that they are a matter of obvious and incontrovertible moral principles that override prudential debate and individual conscience. That is, in its specificity and penchant for pronouncement on matters of particular public policy, the Accra Confession, in the words of Ramsey, presumes "to encompass the prudence of churchmen in their capacities as citizens."[26] As we have seen, it is not obvious or incontrovertible, for instance, that "the root causes of massive threats to life are above all the product of an unjust economic system defended and protected by political and military might" (art. 6).

On the question of whether the Accra Confession is "naturally formulated," we might observe that it was not a confession that itself was produced out of a particular and concrete confessional situation. What Bonhoeffer has in mind is a phenomenon like the Barmen Declaration, which grew out of the Confessing Church's struggle with the Reich church. Only after it was determined by the Confessing Church that its confession was the necessary and appropriate response to the situation in Germany did Bonhoeffer bring the question of the Barmen Declaration to the ecumenical movement in the context of his essay. The genesis of the Accra Confession, by contrast, is not a particular statement of a member church in response to a specific or concrete situation. In this sense, it differs, too, from the Belhar Confession and apartheid in South Africa. The proximate context of the formation of the

Accra Confession is the organization's entry into the *processus confessionis* after the WARC constituency meeting in Kitwe in 1995, but the broader context is not a particular complaint brought about by WARC members, but rather the larger ecumenical movement itself. As Lefever notes, nearly a decade before the Kitwe consultation there was movement within the WCC to determine whether or not the global economic situation amounted to a *status confessionis*. Lefever writes, "In March 1987, the WCC co-sponsored a consultation to determine whether economic justice is a 'confessional' issue, that is, 'one on which a person's position determines whether or not he or she stand within the fellowship of the church.'"[27] This foreshadows the essential faith stance of the Accra Confession, which rejects any who do not agree in its wholesale diagnosis of neoliberal globalization as the cause of world poverty. In this way, the definable progression within the broad ecumenical movement outlined by the critical engagement first from Bonhoeffer, then by Ramsey, and finally by Lefever, appears to be the larger determinative context.

While the validity of confession also involves clarity and theological foundation, the question of truth is ultimately determinative. For Bonhoeffer, the confession must be true in order to be authentic, and these are again points at which the Accra Confession falters. As du Plessis argues convincingly with respect to the Accra statement, the economic narrative of neoliberal globalization put forth by the confession is far from plausible, much less undeniably true. This is equally as applicable for the claims evident in the texts of the broader ecumenical movement, especially those examined from the LWF in chapter 2. As Bonhoeffer writes, there is no possibility of unity without truth.[28]

For Bonhoeffer, the living confession must also include the confession of sin, and the Accra Confession's words in this regard (art. 34) certainly would meet that standard.[29] Even in this case, the confession is used not to unite the sinful together in their common need for God's grace but rather to reinforce the doctrinaire moral conclusions of the document itself. For the Accra Confession, the particular definition of economic justice is what is finally determinative of unity (art. 31).

Ecumenical-Industrial Complex

An aspect of the larger contemporary ecumenical movement's social witness that has emerged in recent years is evidenced in both the concluding section of the Accra Confession as well as the WCRC constitutional clause authorizing the president, the general secretary, or both, to "speak for the World Communion of Reformed Churches between meetings of the General Council."[30] It is, of course, necessary for there to be public representation of the various ecumenical bodies and for them to speak authoritatively, but what we have seen over the last two decades is the abuse of this legitimate purpose of institutional representation. To use Ramsey's language, the legitimate *usus* of ecumenical representation has largely turned into the illegitimate *abusus*.[31]

We see this in the first place in the propensity for institutional figures within the ecumenical movement to speak out publicly on any number of topics, implicitly carrying the weight of the movement's authority with them. In these public statements, the institutional representatives of the ecumenical movement overstep the "moderate and pastoral bounds" of their task.[32] When the president or the general secretary of the World Alliance of Reformed Churches are featured in news accounts, for instance, they are often depicted as representing not only the ecumenical organization but, in so doing, as speaking for the more than 75 million individuals belonging to WARC member churches. The same is true for the public representatives for the LWF and WCC. What Lefever writes of the WCC also holds true for the other ecumenical organizations: "The WCC should not presume to speak *for* the churches, much less for their millions of members. The Council has neither a theological nor an institutional justification for claiming to represent Christians from 100 countries."[33]

Within the last year, for instance, ecumenical leaders have advocated for greater international financial regulation against governmental bailout initiatives of private firms, for debt forgiveness of Third World nations, in defense of liberation theology, against "economic" apartheid (income disparity), and for political action to address climate change.[34] Lefever's questions about the propriety of such institutional representation, whether by an individual in a leadership position or corporately by the organization itself, remain relevant: "Does the WCC, or any particular denomination for that matter, have the right to take a position that runs counter to the majority views of its members? It is generally acknowledged that many WCC pronouncements contradict the majority opinion within the member churches. Does this mean that these pronouncements lack authority?"[35] Do the pronouncements of individual leaders of the ecumenical movement lack authority when they do not reflect the views of the millions of members they claim to represent? It would seem so.

It remains to be seen why leaders who are ostensibly devoted to the service of the church would abuse their position in such ways. One clear incentive for the leaders of the ecumenical movement to cast themselves as representing such large and diverse numbers of Christians is that it provides them credibility in the public square. It is thus a tool that is used to promote the political and social advocacy of the ecumenical movement. This is a use of the platform afforded by the ecumenical movement that reverses the proper emphasis. "The primary obligation of the WCC in the political realm," writes Lefever, "is to speak *to* its member churches, not *for* them."[36] In this way, the ecumenical movement has been focused as much, if not more, for advocating particular views in the public square as it has been for being a resource for the churches themselves.

The ecumenical movement has its own communications body, founded in 1994, devoted to "reporting on ecumenical developments and other news of the churches, and giving religious perspectives on news developments worldwide."[37] The major ecumenical bodies sponsor the network, which serves as the major source of communication both within the global ecumenical movement and for various secular news agencies throughout the world.

The ecumenical movement shares both physical and ideological space across its separate organizations. In the case of the ecumenical-industrial complex, there actually is a physical complex located at the Ecumenical Center in Geneva, housing the Lutheran World Federation, the World Alliance of Reformed Churches, and the World Council of Churches, among many other smaller organizations. These are bodies whose budgets run in the hundreds of millions of dollars and who have a vested interest in the expansion of their influence as far as possible into the public square. Even more, as we have seen from the social pronouncements of the various groups, there is a shared mindset across the bodies of the ecumenical movement. This "social action establishment" (Lefever) or "social action curia" (Ramsey) manifests itself in these institutional decisions to promote specific political viewpoints through the offices of individual leaders, departments, and committees, and to fund the official communications organ of the ecumenical movement, *Ecumenical News International*. This is precisely why Lefever includes among his recommendations aimed at improving the work of the movement that "an effort should be made to recruit a headquarters staff more varied in theological, ethical, and political outlook."[38]

Relevance and Popularization

It remains to establish and explore in more detail the characteristics of this shared mindset or ideology. We have asserted that the basic movement or devolution in ecumenical thought, traced from Bonhoeffer, to Ramsey, to Lefever, to today, has been to first conflate religion with morality and then morality with economics. This final conflation, between ethics and a particular economic worldview is a feature of a discernible tendency in the ecumenical movement to seek relevance and contemporary influence. As Lefever observes: "Trendy clergymen and laymen are often engaged in a thinly disguised rivalry with secular revolutionaries for 'relevance.'"[39] In practice, this kind of engagement has essentially amounted to embracing the secular ideology of the day with an added layer of religiosity, presumably the only aspect of worth the ecumenical movement has to share, but, as Bonhoeffer contends, this kind of accommodation undermines the basis of the Christian gospel itself. He warns: "Do not try to make the Bible relevant. Its relevance is axiomatic.… Do not defend God's Word, but testify to it.… Trust the Word. It is a ship loaded to the very limits of its capacity!"[40]

Instead of trusting the Word, however, in its zeal to gain worldly influence the ecumenical movement has defined itself in terms that would position it to maximize political leverage. The rhetorician Thomas M. Lessl has aptly described how in modern public discourse science and religion compete by embracing points of departure.[41] He identifies both as adopting the "priestly voice," a form of discourse that crosses cultural and class boundaries and attempts to "change the identity of its audiences by nudging them gradually into the symbolic environment of an elite social group." In the case of religion and science, Lessl writes "that the persuasive challenges each institution faces are similar—thus making the materials of religion relevant to the rhetorical objectives of science."[42]

Lessl goes on to describe how the priestly voice of science shares basic features of discourse with religious modes of communication.

In the case of the ecumenical movement, however, the religious institution has adopted the basic stance of science in order to gain a sympathetic hearing in a secular audience.[43] Where the scientist is the undisputed voice of authority, the priest closely mimics the latest scientific trends in an attempt to retain a semblance of relevance. If science has adopted a priestly voice in order to persuade, religion has adopted a scientific voice in order to do the same. In the case of the ecumenical movement, the basic point of scientific departure has in the last fifty years been the social sciences, particularly a brand of economics influenced by Marxist theory.[44] The ecumenical movement has embraced a kind of neo-Marxist economism, as mediated through liberation theology, out of its strife with its secular rivals.

The charge of economism is one that has been leveled against neoclassical economics by its critics, but the reduction of human activity to purely economic causes, or the causes of problems to purely economic analysis, is an error that respects no party line.[45] Ecumenical documents like the Accra Confession, in their reductive and simplistic explanation for global problems as diverse as disease, poverty, and hunger, are univocal in laying the blame on a particular economic cause: neoliberal globalization. By embracing such explanations, the ecumenical movement has uncritically accepted an economistic worldview wholesale, even while it attempts to denounce what it perceives to be the opposite error. The neo-Marxist critique of neoliberalism is no less economistic than that which it proposes to replace. Jettisoned in such a Faustian bargain, however, are particular theological categories such as sin, which have deeper explanatory power for the structural injustices that define life in the fallen world.

More recently, however, the ecumenical movement has left a simple economism behind. It has followed the trajectory of liberation theology itself, which first emphasized a basically economistic or materialistic anthropology but in subsequent development has articulated all manner of liberation theologies, including environmental, ethnic, sexual, and gender revolutions.[46] It is in this development that we can begin to understand the close relationship between the ecumenical critiques of neoliberal economic power and the corresponding complaints about environmental and ecological degradation.[47] Indeed, The Accra Confession manifests this linkage in the "confession" section of the document (arts. 15–36) and explicitly connects "economic injustice and ecological destruction." The connection is also in its judgment that "transnational corporations have plundered the earth and severely damaged the environment" (art. 8). This is the result of these corporations "drive for profit" as well as of the "policy of unlimited growth among industrialized countries."

This judgment against unlimited growth is a direct condemnation of unlimited economic growth, but it is also at the same time an indirect condemnation of unlimited population growth. This implicit misanthropic perception of economic growth and population levels perhaps explains why there has been so little ecumenical proclamation against population-control measures in countries around the world. Writing in a WCC periodical, Gillian Paterson observes, "Population control is a deeply contentious issue, and a huge challenge to ecumenical collaboration." Citing the passionate debates at various United Nations events, from which the ecumenical movement often takes its cues, Paterson writes that "ecumenical groupings, terrified of rocking the boat, will often avoid any overspecific discussion on the subject." Paterson criticizes lack of ecumenical attentiveness to questions of abortion, birth control, and population levels, noting: "In any serious debate about the ethics of health care, it is hard to see how these issues can be ignored."[48] Given the underlying worldview animating ecumenical dialogue on these kinds of issues, however, there is little basis to expect an ethically or theologically sound debate.[49] As Lefever writes: "Taking sides and not taking sides both have moral and political pitfalls. But supporting the wrong side is the worst of all options."[50] Given that, silence on the part of the ecumenical movement on population issues might well be the best realistic possibility to hope for.

It may well be no surprise, though, how the movement from speaking internally to the constituency of the ecumenical movement (what Lessl calls "bardic" discourse), to speaking externally to an audience in the public square (what Lessl calls "priestly" discourse), corresponds with an increasing embrace of secular paradigms of authority, such as the respect afforded to the scientist or the "expert."[51] Indeed, as F. A. Hayek has described in his essay, "The Intellectuals and Socialism," this priestly kind of discourse, which, in Hayek's description is the domain of "the professional secondhand dealers in ideas," is precisely what is needed to communicate an abstract theory such as socialism to the working classes.[52] The ecumenical movement and its leaders have long occupied the class of the intellectuals, having become priestly popularizers of the abstract theories of economics of a particular kind and expert natural scientific research. Hayek's description of the intellectual applies particularly well to the ecumenical spokesperson:

> he need not possess special knowledge of anything in particular, nor need he even be particularly intelligent, to perform his role as intermediary in the spreading of ideas. What qualifies him for his job is the wide range of subjects on which he can readily talk and write, and a position or habits through which he becomes acquainted with new ideas sooner than those to whom he addresses himself.[53]

The ethical ideas being spread in the ecumenical quest for relevance, however, have long since ceased to be those of traditional Christianity.

Notes

1.   Paul Ramsey, *Who Speaks for the Church? A Critique of the 1966 Geneva Conference on Church and Society* (Nashville: Abingdon Press, 1967), 139.

2.   *World Communion of Reformed Churches (WCRC) Constitution* (proposed July 2009), art. I.

3.   *WCRC Constitution*, art. II.

4.   *WCRC Constitution*, art. VIII.A.

5.   *WCRC Constitution*, art. X.F.2.

6.   *WCRC Constitution*, art. XI.

7.   *WCRC Constitution*, art. XII.A.

8.   *WCRC Constitution*, art. XIII.B.

9.   *WCRC Constitution*, art. XVI.

10. For background on the World Alliance of Reformed Churches, see Alan P. F. Sell, *A Reformed, Evangelical, Catholic Theology: The Contribution of the World Alliance of Reformed Churches, 1875–1982* (Grand Rapids: Eerdmans, 1991). See also Marcel Pradervand, *A Century of Service: A History of the World Alliance of Reformed Churches, 1875–1975* (Grand Rapids: Eerdmans, 1975).

11. See, for instance, *Power to Resist and Courage to Hope: Caribbean Churches Living out the Accra Confession*, ed. Patricia Sheerattan-Bisnauth (Geneva: World Alliance of Reformed Churches and Caribbean and North America Area Council, 2009); and "Message from the Global Dialogue on the Accra Confession," (Johannesburg, South Africa, September 2009).

12. Kitwe statement quoted in Milan Opocensky, "Address of the General Secretary," World Alliance of Reformed Churches 23rd

General Council (Debrecen, Hungary, 1997). References to the Accra Confession itself will be noted parenthetically throughout this chapter.

13. See Opocensky, "Address of the General Secretary."

14. Stan du Plessis, "How Can You Be a Christian and an Economist? The Meaning of the Accra Declaration for Today," *Stellenbosch Economic Working Papers* (February 2010): 1–14.

15. du Plessis, "How Can You Be a Christian and an Economist?" 3.

16. du Plessis, "How Can You Be a Christian and an Economist?" 4.

17. It should be noted here that the LWF documentation cites the Washington Consensus as a specific example of neoliberal economic theory. See "'For the Healing of the World,' Excerpts from the 2003 LWF Assembly Message," in *Communion, Responsibility, Accountability: Responding as a Lutheran Communion to Neoliberal Globalization*, ed. Karen L. Bloomquist (Geneva: Lutheran World Federation, 2004), 125.

18. du Plessis, "How Can You Be a Christian and an Economist?" 5.

19. du Plessis, "How Can You Be a Christian and an Economist?" 7.

20. du Plessis, "How Can You Be a Christian and an Economist?" 3.

21. du Plessis, "How Can You Be a Christian and an Economist?" 7.

22. du Plessis, "How Can You Be a Christian and an Economist?" 11. Compare Gerard Berghoef and Lester DeKoster, *Liberation Theology: The Church's Future Shock* (Grand Rapids: Christian's Library Press, 1984), 37: "Ideology inscribes its visions on the sky and upon the heart, and drowns the voice of conscience in the roar of the mob." See also J. A. Emerson Vermaat, *The World Council of Churches and Politics, 1975–1986* (Lanham: Freedom House, 1989), 102: "The Council's concern for Third World poverty, economic debt, hunger and racism, for example, is a valuable addition to the international attempts to aid millions of people. To blame reflexively the West in general, and democratic capitalism in particular, for problems in the Third

World is both unworthy of a worldwide church organization and unproductive toward resolving Third World ills."

23. Dietrich Bonhoeffer, "The Confessing Church and the Ecumenical Movement," in *No Rusty Swords: Letters, Lectures and Notes 1928–1936*, trans. Edwin H. Robertson and John Bowden, ed. Edwin H. Robertson (New York: Harper & Row, 1965), 328.

24. Bonhoeffer, "The Confessing Church and the Ecumenical Movement," 335.

25. Bonhoeffer, "The Confessing Church and the Ecumenical Movement," 338.

26. Ramsey, *Who Speaks for the Church?* 15.

27. Ernest W. Lefever, *Nairobi to Vancouver: The World Council of Churches and the World, 1975–87* (Washington, D.C.: Ethics and Public Policy Center, 1987), 61.

28. Bonhoeffer, "The Confessing Church and the Ecumenical Movement," 336.

29. See Bonhoeffer, "The Confessing Church and the Ecumenical Movement," 338: "In the face of this picture it [the ecumenical movement] will experience afresh the whole need of its own decision and in this situation its confession will be first a *confession of sin.*"

30. *WCRC Constitution*, art. X.F.2.

31. Ramsey, *Who Speaks for the Church?* 17.

32. Bonhoeffer, "The Confessing Church and the Ecumenical Movement," 328.

33. Lefever, *Amsterdam to Nairobi* 59.

34. Stephen Brown, "Faith Leaders Say G20 Must Deal with 'Greed' of Financial System," *Ecumenical News International* (March 30, 2009); Stephen Brown, "Global Protestant Leader Derides Credit Crunch 'Rescue Packages,'" *Ecumenical News International* (May 28, 2009); World Council of Churches Central Committee, "Statement on Eco-Justice and Ecological

Debt," issued September 2, 2009 (Geneva: World Council of Churches, 2009); Walter Altmann, "Liberation Theology Is Alive and Well," *WCC Features* (November 16, 2009); Rogate R. Mshana, "The Current Economic Crisis, Its Causes, Its Impact and Possible Alternatives," a lecture at the 33rd Assembly of the United Congregational Church of Southern Africa, August 24, 2009, Molepolole, Botswana (Geneva: World Council of Churches, 2009); and Peter Kenny, "World Church Leader Urges Other Faiths to Join Christians on Climate," *Ecumenical News International* (February 23, 2010). This brief survey could be augmented exponentially.

35. Lefever, *Amsterdam to Nairobi*, 10.

36. Lefever, *Amsterdam to Nairobi*, 58.

37. Ecumenical News International, "Introducing ENI," http://www.eni.ch/information/introduction.shtml.

38. Lefever, *Amsterdam to Nairobi*, 57.

39. Lefever, *Amsterdam to Nairboi*, 50.

40. Quoted in Eberhard Bethge, *Dietrich Bonhoeffer: A Biography*, rev. ed., trans. Eric Mosbacher et al. (Minneapolis: Fortress Press, 2000), 442.

41. Thomas M. Lessl, "The Priestly Voice," *Quarterly Journal of Speech* 75 (May 1989): 183–97.

42. Lessl, "The Priestly Voice," 188.

43. See also Eugene Y. Lowe Jr., "From Social Gospel to Social Science at the University of Wisconsin," in *The Church's Public Role*, ed. Dieter T. Hessel (Grand Rapids: Eerdmans, 1993), 226–44.

44. On "Economics as Faith," see Samuel J. Gregg, *Economic Thinking for the Theologically Minded* (Lanham: University Press of America, 2001), 53–55.

45. On the limits of disciplinary conceptual models, see Edward J. O'Boyle, "Requiem for *Homo Economicus*," *Journal of Markets & Morality* 10, no. 2 (Fall 2007): 321–37.

46. For a critical engagement of black liberation theology, for instance, see Anthony B. Bradley, *Liberating Black Theology: The Bible and the Black Experience in America* (Wheaton: Crossway, 2010).

47. For a recent study of these two paradigms in the North American context, see Robert H. Nelson, *The New Holy Wars: Economic Religion vs. Environmental Religion in Contemporary America* (University Park: Pennsylvania State University Press, 2010).

48. Gillian Paterson, "Chapter Four: Brave New World," in "The CMC Story, 1968–1998," *Contact*, nos. 161/162 (June-July and August-September 1998): 51.

49. See, for instance, James B. Martin-Schramm, *Population Perils and the Churches' Response* (Geneva: World Council of Churches, 1997).

50. Lefever, *Amsterdam to Nairobi*, 54.

51. For an example of how this often leads to a kind of statism, see Alasdair MacIntyre, *After Virtue*, 2nd ed. (Notre Dame: University of Notre Dame Press, 2003), 85: "Government insists more and more that its civil servants themselves have the kind of education that will qualify them as experts. It more and more recruits those who claim to be experts into its civil service. And it characteristically recruits too the heirs of the nineteenth-century reformers. Government itself becomes a hierarchy of bureaucratic managers, and the major justification advanced for the intervention of government in society is the contention that government has resources of competence which most citizens do not possess."

52. F. A. Hayek, "The Intellectuals and Socialism," in *The Intellectuals: A Controversial Portrait*, ed. George B. de Huszar (Glencoe: The Free Press, 1960), 371.

53. Hayek, "The Intellectuals and Socialism," 371.

4

WORLD COUNCIL OF CHURCHES (WCC)

*Does the World Council of Churches have
a future? Does it deserve to have a future?
Or has it already passed into a state of
benign ineffectiveness?*[1]

—Ernest W. Lefever

Background and Structure

The World Council of Churches (WCC) is the largest and
most diverse of organizations in the ecumenical movement,
made up of 349 member churches in more than 110 countries
worldwide, representing over 560 million Christians. The
WCC was officially formed in 1948 in the aftermath of World
War II and identifies itself as "a fellowship of churches which
confess the Lord Jesus Christ as God and Saviour according
to the scriptures and therefore seek to fulfil together their
common calling to the glory of the one God, Father, Son and
Holy Spirit."[2] The basic self-understanding of the WCC is that
it exists "to serve the one ecumenical movement" and "to call

one another to visible unity in one faith and in one eucharistic fellowship, expressed in worship and common life in Christ, through witness and service to the world, and to advance towards that unity in order that the world may believe."[3]

The highest authoritative body in the WCC is the assembly, which meets every seven years.[4] The latest meeting of the assembly was held in 2006 in Porto Alegre, Brazil, with the petitionary theme, "God, in your grace, transform the world." The Tenth Assembly is scheduled to be held in 2013 in Busan, South Korea. The WCC constitution also provides for the central committee, which is "responsible for implementing the policies adopted by the assembly and shall exercise the functions of the assembly itself delegated to it by the assembly between its meetings, except its power to amend this constitution and to allocate or alter the allocation of the membership of [the] central committee."[5] The assembly elects the presidents of the WCC, who serve between assemblies and are "to promote ecumenism and to interpret the work of the World Council of Churches, especially in their respective regions." Up to eight presidents may serve simultaneously.[6] The central committee appoints the general secretary, who serves as "the chief executive officer of the World Council" and who normally serves for a term of five years.[7]

Of special note is the section of the WCC rules that outlines the specific nature of the authority of public statements by the assembly and the central committee. The WCC rules also recognize the right of various officers and staff of the WCC to issue such statements when the assembly or central committee is not in session.[8] The WCC reserves the right and responsibility to "issue statements on any situation or concern with which the Council or its constituent churches may be confronted."[9] The scope of WCC public statements is in this way virtually unlimited. The authority of these statements, by contrast, is understood to "consist only in the weight which they carry by their own truth and wisdom, and the publishing of such statements shall not be held to imply that the World Council as such has, or can have, any constitutional authority over the constituent churches or right to speak for them."[10] The document under examination here is the Report of the Public Issues Committee, presented and adopted by the Ninth General Assembly in 2006, and that therefore represents an authoritative institutional expression of the perspective of the World Council of Churches.

Report of the Public Issues Committee (2006)

The report of the public issues committee presented to the WCC general assembly in 2006 is composed of eight sections. In addition to the introduction, following sections address (1) Latin America, (2) responsibility to protect vulnerable populations, (3) UN reform, (4) terrorism, (5) water, (6) nuclear arms, and (7) people of other faiths. When the public issues committee (PIC) first presented the agenda for its 2006 General Assembly report a number of other specific issues were put forth by assembly participants as deserving specific attention, including the question of poverty. The PIC report observes that "poverty is indeed a major issue in our world and fighting poverty a priority for the World Council of Churches," and goes on to highlight the statements from the eighth assembly in Harare, Zimbabwe, that the "reality of unequal distribution of power and wealth, of poverty and exclusion challenges the cheap language of our global shared community." The report judges that "the lack of a strong ethical and moral approach in responding to poverty is sinful in the eyes of God," and, observing that the challenge of the WCC response to poverty "must be an intentional on-going process," commends three specific statements within its report "where the issue of poverty is address." These sections are the statements on Latin America, reforming the United Nations, and water for life.[11]

Latin America

The statements on various topics in the PIC report contain two basic parts. The first details the origins of the statement and the basis for whatever response is recommended. The second section outlines the resolutions taken by the ninth assembly in which the report sections were adopted and various actions endorsed. The statement on Latin America traces the history of colonialism and brings this brief narrative into contemporary context by noting that the political independence achieved in the nineteenth century "left different nations still economically dependent" (1.3). In addition to this legacy of economic dependence, the nations of Latin America are the victims of "irresponsible policies by governments and multinational corporations which have irreparably damaged their environment" (1.5).

These linked causes have resulted in a number of deleterious economic consequences. For instance, observes the PIC report: "Unjust distribution of wealth, natural resources and opportunities has generated poverty, which dramatically affects the region. According to UN statistics, now as for decades, more than 40 percent of the population still live in poverty, while 20 percent live in extreme poverty" (1.6). There are of course wide variations between the situations of different nations in Latin America, but, as the report states: "Even in those countries where poverty is relatively less, the gap between the rich and the poor is enormous and the distribution of wealth continues to be unjust" (1.6). Reiterating the connection between economic poverty and environmental destruction, the report contends that "poverty is unacceptable in a region which is extremely rich in natural resources." Even so, "the tragedy is that these have often been exploited in a way that has destroyed the environment through, for example, the contamination of rivers in large areas. Indeed the whole planet is threatened through the deforestation of the Amazonian region" (1.7).

In attempting to describe the role of the Christian church in addressing the situation in Latin America, the PIC report specifically raises the question of international debt. In this case, "churches in the region have clearly stated the debt is unjust, illegitimate and immoral because it had been contracted during dictatorships with the complicity of international financial institutions and has already been paid." The debt has ongoing effects, in that "the need to continue to pay the service of the debt has prevented the implementation of effective social policies in most of the countries, seriously affecting education, health and work conditions (1.7)." The basic point here is that the International Financial Institutions, in collusion with corrupt governments and the international hegemony of the United States and its empire, have functioned to keep Latin American countries in a state of economic subservience.

However, beyond the specific question of debt relief, the churches and the ecumenical movement have another role to play in combating injustice. The PIC report cites the record of Latin American churches in the development of liberation theology as a responsible response to injustice. In the report's narrative,

> this particular consideration for the poor, the marginalized and the excluded in different societies throughout history has been at the origins of the particular theological approach known as Liberation Theology. Strongly incarnated in the social struggles of the 1960s and 1970s, more recently it has expanded its foci towards the economic, ecological, gender and inter-religious dimensions. Therefore, nurtured in this theological methodology rooted in a deep spiritual experience, Latin American Christianity has become deeply involved in defending, caring and celebrating life in its multiple manifestations, recognising God's presence in every life expression and especially in human life. This experience has been a gift of God to the whole Church. (1.19)

On the basis of the strength of this narrative and its reception at the general assembly, the PIC report was adopted by a resolution that included a statement urging "the international community, the states and International Financial Institutions to recognize the illegitimacy of the external debt that burdens the region." The resolution also called on these institutions "to revise the rationale of free trade agreements in order to effectively respond to the needs of the population and to the concerns expressed recently by the churches in the region regarding the consequences for peasants, workers and communities' rights, the environment and citizen's participation" (1.g).

Reforming the United Nations

The section of the PIC report addressed to the need for reform of the United Nations (UN) focuses more broadly on the role that the ecumenical movement is called to play on the international stage in addition to the particular contribution at the regional level as in Latin America. In this way, the PIC report states that "the churches, together with the wider civil society, carry a responsibility to shape the public opinion and to generate the political will for multilateral co-operative action that is needed for the UN to succeed in its mission" (4.1). The PIC report outlines a number of ways in which the deliberative process at the United Nations is flawed or insufficient. Even so, the report judges that "in spite of weaknesses of the UN and failures of governments to cooperate through its forum it is still the best instrument that we have to respond to the contemporary challenges" (4.6). The report goes on to specifically note the Millennium Development Goals (MDGs) as well as pledges to forgive or cancel "unpayable and illegitimate debt" as positive reasons for optimism regarding the utility of the United Nations (4.6).

Citing the radical paradigm shift experienced at the conclusion of the Cold War and the subsequent rapid globalization of trade and technological advance (4.5), however, the PIC report contends that "the UN and member states … engage in a serious process of reform in order to retain the capacity to respond to the basic mandate of the UN and to the aspirations of the people of the world. The reform process must continue to go beyond the framework of the UN organization and aim at improving global governance based on the principle of multilateralism" (4.7). The context for the following judgments about necessary reforms are based especially on the 2005 UN World Summit, which recognized that "peace/security, development/social and economic justice and the implementation of human rights are inseparably linked" (4.8). Indeed, "the fact that the outcome document of the 2005 UN World Summit recognizes the inseparable linkage of the three pillars of security, development and human rights speaks for determined efforts to strengthen organizational and policy coherence in the UN system across borders and between specialized institutions, interests and constituencies" (4.10).

In this context, the ecumenical movement in general and the WCC in particular understands its role to facilitate and advocate for the specific reforms of the United Nations that would allow it to meet its varied responsibilities. The PIC report notes particularly that "the WCC was the first organization to propose a target for official development assistance, of two percent of national income." The significance of this is that it provides a model for other churches to do the same as their abilities allow. "It is vital that member churches in donor countries continue to be strong advocates to their governments and the public of sustaining or increasing aid to the UN target of 0.7 percent of GDP without harmful economic conditions," contends the PIC report. "Combined with more just trade policies and faster and deeper reduction of official debt, it is possible to sustain development and poverty reduction to fulfill the MDGs, and even move beyond these important limited goals" (1.12). The primary mode of action for the ecumenical movement in this context is a kind of prophetic advocacy, constantly pushing the United Nations and other international institutions to live up to the demands of the contemporary global situation.

The fundamental lesson of the PIC report on the need for reform of the United Nations is the critical role that the ecumenical movement must play in any improvement efforts. The report states, "The unique role that religions or religious organizations could play in addressing conflict, and working for peace, human rights and ending poverty is not yet fully realized." Indeed, "There is an urgent need for the UN and member states to strengthen the capacity to deal with the growing interaction between religion and politics." It is here that there is a corresponding responsibility, "an urgent need for the churches and the WCC to strengthen their own capacities to continue and improve their engagements with the UN" (1.14).

The Assembly's adoption of this report included the reiteration of the need to empower the United Nations and other international governance institutions to enforce their decisions and resolutions. Thus, the assembly's resolution argues that the "UN Economic and Social Council should be enabled to hold finance ministers, meetings on global macro-economic management, to more actively address environmental issues integrated with social and economic issues and to hold the International Financial Institutions to account." Moreover, "commitments made by governments in financing for development, towards meeting the Millennium Development Goals, debt cancellation and for sustainable development should be seen as binding and the UN has to be given instruments to ensure their implementation" (4.f). In support of these efforts, the assembly's resolution calls member churches to perform the necessary tasks of advocacy, admonishment, and encouragement. Churches are "to work with member states to make the UN an initiator and a global monitor for management of natural resources and public goods and for strengthening the mechanisms to ensure that transnational corporations are held accountable to global standards" (4.g).

Water for Life

One particular area in which such global governance bodies must pay particular attention, contends the PIC report, is the protection of sources of fresh water. Outlining some of the causes and effects of a crisis in the availability of fresh water, the PIC report states that "biodiversity is also threatened by the depletion and pollution of fresh water resources or through impacts of large dams, large scale mining and hot cultures (irrigation) whose construction often involves the forced displacement of people and disruption of the ecosystem." The environmental causes are of the utmost importance, since "the integrity and balance of the ecosystem is crucial for the access to water. Forests build an indispensable part in the ecosystem of water and must be protected" (5.2).

In terms of addressing the economic causes of the shortage of water, the PIC reports: "The crisis is aggravated by climate change and further deepened by strong economic interests. Water is increasingly treated as a commercial good, subject to market conditions" (5.2). The commodification of water violates justice, because "access to water is indeed a basic human right" (5.5). The PIC statement concludes with encouragement for member churches and other ecumenical organizations to dialogue and engage institutions at all levels. Such engagement, with other religious groups, NGOs, governments, corporations, and multinational institutions, is "essential to promote the significance of the right to water and to point to alternative ways of living, which are more respectful of ecological processes and more sustainable in the longer term" (5.6).

The assembly resolution adopted the section on water, emphasizing the need for the WCC to undertake "advocacy efforts for development of legal instruments and mechanisms that guarantee the implementation of the right to water as a fundamental human right at the local, national, regional and international levels" (5.c). In addition, there is an emphasis on local engagement, the support of "community based initiatives whose objectives are to enable local people to exercise responsible control, manage and regulate water resources and prevent the exploitation for commercial purposes" (5.e).

Analysis

The report of the public issues committee to the ninth general assembly of the WCC in 2006 and its adoption by the assembly testify to a pervasive perspective on poverty shared across the movement. In the context of similar pronouncements by other groups, we see that the whole-cloth economic narrative of neo-Marxist ideology is spread over the entire ecumenical movement, from the LWF, to the WARC, to the WCC. As Lefever put it in 1987: "For the past decade and more, the leaders of the World Council of Churches have addressed selective aspects of the economic question, almost exclusively from an ideological perspective that asserts the superiority of a government-administered economy over the market. The Council's pronouncements assume a cause-effect relationship between Western capitalism and imperialism on the one hand, and poverty, oppression, and militarism on the other."[12] Very little has changed in the last two decades.

In the PIC report on Latin America, contemporary economic challenges in the region are traced to the legacy of Western colonialism. In this contemporary context, however, the difference is the globalized economy and the international financial institutions (IFIs), such as the International Monetary Fund (IMF) and the World Bank. These institutions are understood to be proxies by which First World nations conspire to keep developing nations in economic bondage—a form of neocolonialism.

The PIC report explicitly endorses the standard approach of the WCC to this situation in the form of liberation theology, which when put into action has led to a Latin American experience that "has been a gift of God to the whole Church" (1.19). Recently the Reverend Dr. Walter Altmann, moderator of the WCC Central Committee and president of the Evangelical Church of the Lutheran Confession in Brazil issued a statement articulating the contemporary vigor of liberation theology.[13] In this brief statement, Altmann provides a compelling analysis of the dynamic nature of liberation theology. Thus, he writes: "As a contextual approach, aimed at critically reflecting on the praxis of God's people, liberation theology was never intended to become a static, dogmatic theoretical construction. Its intention was not to highlight a neglected theological theme, but rather to propose a new way of doing theology." Liberation theology originally took its point of departure in an economic critique of market economies, but from this basic perspective followed a series of other kinds of social criticisms. "At the outset it focused on the living conditions of the poor," writes Altmann, "later on it incorporated other issues, like indigenous peoples, racism, gender inequalities and ecology." The key word here is *incorporated*.

It is true that liberation theology has not remained static since its original classical expression in the 1960s. It is equally true, despite Altmann's claims to the contrary, that it has never abandoned its core perspective, the fundamentally neo-Marxist critique of market economics. The continuing vitality of liberation theology in its variety of forms underscores how its accommodation of the neo-Marxist critique amounted to the formation of an all-encompassing world-and-life view (*Weltanschaaung*). It has simply taken the intervening decades for implications of the inner dynamic of this essentially economistic worldview to be fully worked out.[14] As Altmann concludes, "above all, liberation theology continues to be very much alive and well within civil society movements and Christian base communities." In this way, liberation theology is a kind of theological Hydra, finding numerous novel expressions in each concrete context. This bespeaks its continuing vitality, as witnessed to by Altmann, as well as to its comprehensive explanatory claims.

In this way, Lefever's critique of the WCC's revolutionary logic continues to apply. Lefever writes that "in practical terms, this doctrine calls for a class struggle against feudalism, multinational corporations, and Western imperialism along the lines of V. I. Lenin's pregnant dictum: 'Imperialism is the last stage of capitalism.'"[15] We have now seen these same features in the social statements of each of the three major ecumenical organizations. Lefever writes: "Liberation theology identifies itself closely with the Marxist-Leninist doctrine and practice of 'national liberation,' which insists that unjust political and economic structures (capitalism and imperialism) can be eliminated only by protracted pressure, including revolutionary violence."[16] In our limited survey of contemporary ecumenical statements, we have seen little in the way of blatant agitation for revolutionary violence, although the Accra Confession does declare "that the church is called to confess, witness and act, even though the authorities and human law might forbid them, and punishment and suffering be the consequence (Acts 4.18ff)" (art. 35). In isolation, this kind of proposition can be understood simply as the uncontroversial assertion that human beings are ultimately accountable to a higher law and a higher standard than merely the will of the government. But within the broader context of the ecumenical movement's social witness, it seems to carry a more sinister connotation. It may well be that the WCC has decided that the more prudent course of action is to cease direct funding of revolutionary groups in the Third World.[17] Instead, it is pursuing the more promising, and more publicly respectable, method of engaging the United Nations and other institutions of global governance.

The WCC and the UN

The section of the PIC report on the possibility for reform of the United Nations is illuminating for the basic approach to political advocacy that the WCC takes today. In the WCC's view, the promise of the United Nations lies in its potential to embody a true international governing body, including the power to enforce its decisions and decrees. It is clear that the WCC understands itself as having a critical apologetic role for the United Nations and its public mission: "The churches, together with the wider civil society, carry a responsibility to shape the public opinion and to generate the political will for multilateral co-operative action that is needed for the UN to succeed in its mission" (4.1). This underscores the task of popularization as outlined in the previous chapter.[18]

In describing its relationship with the United Nations, the WCC asserts that the United Nations, just as the ecumenical movement in general, "finds itself at a critical juncture" with respect to the "rapid spread of globalization" (4.5). In recounting the recent achievements of the United Nations, it is clear that a great deal of hope is placed in the organization: "In its 60-year history the UN and its specialized agencies have been able to strengthen the international rule of law, resolve many conflicts (e.g., in Kampuchea, East Timor, Namibia, and Liberia), resettle millions of refugees, raise the level of literacy, support education for all, introduce basic health care, fight poverty and respond to countless emergencies as well as natural and man-made disasters" (4.6). There is little, it seems, that the UN cannot do.

The United Nations would be able to do much more if the WCC were able to assist it in achieving the kind of authority necessary to demand adherence. Thus, the WCC focuses its advocacy on "improving global governance based on the principle of multilateralism," by which it means especially the empowerment of the United Nations to enforce compliance (4.7). These kinds of implications of the PIC report are confirmed by the content of the assembly's resolution adopting the report. The report was adopted for the intention "to advance the objective of a more effective United Nations" (4.a), noting that this effectiveness "depends on accountable and inclusive democratic decision-making that does not sideline small, less powerful, and economically deprived members" (4.b). In addition, "the success of UN reform is judged in terms of the capacity of the UN to change the situation of people on the ground and make practical positive difference and an improvement to their comprehensive wellbeing" (4.b). All well and good.

However, the WCC insinuates itself into the political workings of the United Nations to such an extent that it views the United Nations as a primary audience, its own particular mission field, by affirming "the dedication of the WCC to be present and visible at the UN" (4.b). Moreover, to effectively implement effective success of the nature outlined above, the WCC advocates empowering the United Nations to enforce agreements made by member nations. Thus, "commitments made by governments in financing for development, towards meeting the Millennium Development Goals, debt cancellation and for sustainable development should be seen as binding and the UN has to be given instruments to ensure their implementation" (4.f). Moreover, the WCC urges its member churches to help their governments "make the UN an initiator and a global monitor for management of natural resources and public goods and for strengthening the mechanisms to ensure that transnational corporations are held accountable to global standards" (4.g).

Proposals of this kind are little different from those calls for a New International Economic Order that Lefever finds in the WCC proposals of the 1970s and 1980s. As Lefever writes, "The WCC's solution for the world's 'maldistribution of wealth' and oppressive structures has been a New International Economic Order (NIEO). The NIEO proposal originated in the early 1970s in the United Nations, where Third World governments were calling for a global redistribution of resources."[19] Lefever concludes that "the Council position on the world economic situation is a version of 'dependency theory.' Based on a largely Marxist-inspired economic model, this theory asserts that the Third World is exploited for the economic gain of the industrialized world."[20] This characterization applies equally well to the more recent PIC report under consideration here. The underlying consistency of the kind of international advocacy in the WCC over the last forty years belies Altmann's depiction that liberation theology as expressed in the ecumenical movement has moved beyond Marxist economic analysis. Instead, it supports the interpretation put forward in this critical engagement, in which the globalized form of Marxist economic theory (neo-Marxism) is the fundamental basis for other varieties of social liberation, whether ethnic, ecological, or sexual.

Water and Human Rights

The PIC report on water manifests an important aspect of the debate over justice, specifically regarding the issue of human rights. As the WCC asserts, "access to water is indeed a basic human right" (5.5). By itself, however, agreement to this proposition does not commit anyone to affirming a particular perspective on what ways such a right is to be respected and protected.

In continuity with its basic approach on other issues, the WCC opposes what it understands to be the commodification of water, in which it is "increasingly treated as a commercial good, subject to market conditions" (5.2). The ecumenical analysis takes as a fundamental assumption that "basic human rights" like access to water are best, and perhaps solely, the domain of the government, both in terms of protection as well as in terms of provision.[21]

It is not obvious at all that market conditions are not typically the most efficient way of allocating precious resources. *Most efficient* in this sense is not to be confused with *perfect*. Generally speaking, however, markets are the best means, from a variety of perspectives, of getting resources to where they need to be with the least amount of interference, delay, and cost. Basic human needs present a special challenge, to be sure, but it is a perverse kind of Christianity that looks first to the government to provide for those whose needs are not being met in a market system. This is a kind of Christianity that substitutes advocacy for charity, that prefers government taxes to the church's tithe. As Claar and Klay write: "Whenever community needs are not fully met by markets and existing government programs, Christians should consider how to bridge the gaps—whether for basic drugs or childcare."[22] Most often, the most obedient way to bridge the gap is to serve the person in need directly. Indeed, "Christians have the calling, the means and the gifts to provide services ranging from education to care for persons with physical and mental limitations."[23] Too often, however, charity has become confused and conflated with coerced governmental distribution.

There is little controversy about the scale of the global problem of access to clean water, but there is healthy and helpful debate about the best ways to maximize the availability of access to water. In 2004, Frank Rijsberman, then director general of the International Water Management Institute in Colombo, Sri Lanka, wrote a paper arguing that "future investments should not be focused on a narrow technology-based approach implemented primarily through national government. Instead, the focus should be on a combination of interventions that combine technology, institutions and (social) marketing, implemented through decentralized organizations closely linked to, or directed by, the users."[24] A panel of internationally recognized economists ranked a number of projects aimed at improving access to clean water as "likely to be highly cost-effective," and these included proposals aimed specifically at using microcredit and other market-based tools for implementation.[25] Only an ideological approach would rule out the possibilities of such endeavors in favor of governmental action.

As fruitful as a rights-based approach to public discourse can be, at some point the dialogue will founder on differing concepts of the human person upon which those rights are based. Are human beings primarily stewards of God's creation who exercise their stewardship responsibilities in the form of rights and responsibilities for property? Or, are human beings primarily victims or supplicants who must depend on the provision of government for their well-being? It is here that the question of anthropology becomes central.

Anthropology and Economics

Theologian John Schneider has written a masterful essay exploring the anthropological implications of an affirmation or denial of market economies.[26] Schneider provides a convincing defense of the market economy against the claim that it is essentially antihuman and furthermore articulates a positive case for viewing markets as fundamentally supportive of a biblical anthropology. Schneider's analysis is particularly helpful because the positions he engages match so closely with those we have already seen represented in the statements of the ecumenical movement.

In general, Schneider's defense of the humaneness of the market economy is aimed against those claims that regard such systems or cultures as consisting in human beings who are "caught in desire for things, animated by a driving lust for money, and held captive to alienating roles." As Schneider notes, "this is not a pretty picture of our humanity as it inevitably evolves under capitalism." But on Schneider's account, we need not be overly troubled by this "abysmal picture," in part because it is inaccurate, both in terms of its depiction of human nature as well as of the character of market economies.[27]

In the negative account of capitalism, human beings are viewed as captives, slaves, and victims. This is in part because the account's only input is essentially materialistic. It does nothing to show regard for *other* aspects of human nature (e.g., spiritual, emotional, mental). Drawing on a number of sociological and philosophical sources, Schneider describes the positive account of human engagement with market economies as consisting in the fullness of human *character*. "The free, creative, and economically awakened individual is the key to the whole delicate thing," he writes.[28] Schneider summarizes the positive account of market economies and the human person in this way: "On the side of capitalism, it seems to be a cultural environment that is unusually open to Christianity in realizing its ontology of personal calling. On the other side, it seems that Christianity has a human ontology that can give distinctly Christian and human shape to the cultural dispositions and habits of capitalism."[29] If we understand the essence of the human person to consist in the image of God (*imago Dei*), and we understand this image to consist in our faculties and our responsible use of these gifts as stewards in the world, we have a much fuller and more comprehensive picture of the dynamic relationship between human beings and markets.

The resulting picture, then, is that Marxist and neo-Marxist analysis are bad economics because, in large part, they are bad anthropologies. They do not account for the biblical picture of human nature. By contrast, a biblical appreciation for the image of God in its comprehensive sense "greatly strengthens confidence that genuine humanity can thrive under capitalism and that we can engage it constructively in authentically Christian theological terms."[30]

Hope for Reform?

It remains to be addressed whether or not this critical engagement, as we near its conclusion, has any basis for optimism that its criticisms might have some positive effect on the future development of the ecumenical movement's social witness. There is at least some reason in the shared line of critique from Bonhoeffer, to Ramsey, to Lefever for doubt. As we have seen, the progression of this critique becomes increasingly focused on the particular ideological development of the ecumenical movement. It moves from a basically ecclesiological criticism in Bonhoeffer, to a basically ethical concern in Ramsey, to an economic critique in Lefever. At the conclusion of his first book, Lefever includes a number of concrete suggestions for reform of the movement.[31] By the time Lefever finishes his second book, his hopefulness has been severely dampened. Thus, he asks: "Does the World Council of Churches have a future? Does it deserve to have a future? Or has it already passed into a state of benign ineffectiveness?"[32]

Lefever judges that the WCC is largely ineffective, in that "the World Council of Churches is seldom taken seriously. Most consequential religious, academic, political, and business leaders have long since recognized the irresponsibility of the WCC's advice,[33] but this ineffectiveness is in no sense *benign*. The WCC continues to be "influential in perverse ways, primarily as a continuing source of confusion and as an active supporter of revolutionary elites, both religious and secular."[34] This is what Lefever assesses in terms of the

WCC's positive influence. In contemporary contexts, there are reasons to believe that Lefever's analysis continues to be true, but the commitment of the WCC and the broader ecumenical movement to the empowerment of the United Nations should not be discounted either.[35] In addition, the development of the ecumenical-industrial complex has increased the ability for the ecumenical movement to diffuse its influence as a source of confusion.

On the negative side, Lefever criticizes the WCC for its squander of moral authority. "When speaking to the churches," writes Lefever, "the WCC has failed to instruct them adequately about the real issues in a dangerous world, the agonizing decisions that confront statesmen, and the limited choices that citizens have. It has presented a highly skewed picture of reality, one distorted by the bankrupt ideology and practice of Marxism."[36] Because of his diagnosis of the neo-Marxist ideology as endemic to the ecumenical movement's social witness, Lefever bemoans significant hope that reform is possible.

While expressing "hope that radical reform—a return to the principles of the 1948 Assembly—may still be possible," Lefever concludes that he sees "little hope for significant constructive change in the near future." He is "inclined to look elsewhere in the Christian community for the development and practice of a morally sound and politically responsible approach to the perplexing problems of this world."[37] This is a point that bears further examination. It is indeed the case that the vast majority of ecumenical activity takes place outside the official purview or unofficial influence of the institutions of the LWF, WCRC, or WCC. There are, in fact, many more ecumenical institutions of various sizes and compositions that also form parts of the movement. In addition to these other institutions and efforts, Christians engaged organically in social and civil life undertake ecumenical activity in a plethora of ways.

Lefever invokes the words of William Temple, "the late Archbishop of Canterbury and a pioneer ecumenical leader," who said that "nine-tenths of the work of the Church in the world is done by Christian people fulfilling responsibilities and performing tasks which are not part of the official system of the Church at all."[38] In addition to the work of the church in the world, there is also a kind of mere ecumenism that is a basic feature of the twofold reality of the church as institution and organism. When Christians from different denominations and traditions, outside of the institutional church, have conversations and dialogue, engage in forms of prayer and worship, and do works of charity and justice together, they are engaging in meaningful ecumenical endeavors. Lefever himself expressed the conviction that new ecumenical institutions and partnerships would form, citing "a combination of contemporary forces, including Protestant evangelicals, sectors of the Roman Catholic Church, and leaders of the Lutheran tradition."[39] Undoubtedly the coalition recently formed in support the Manhattan Declaration, focusing on questions of life, marriage, and religious liberty, manifests realization of the kind of hope expressed here by Lefever, but there is special reason for hope in other institutions and efforts, including those working primarily from the perspective of mission and evangelism, such as the Lausanne Movement.[40]

In this way, it is true that the hope for a vigorous, effective, and obedient ecumenical social witness is not coextensive with the institutional ecumenical movement itself—still less with the three institutions surveyed in this engagement. Even so, this present critical engagement has been undertaken with the conviction that reform of the ecumenical movement, in the institutional expressions represented by the LWF, the WCRC, and the WCC is possible. As long as the movement retains a formal basis as represented in the statements of the report from the Amsterdam Assembly in 1948, "The Church and the Disorder of Society," there is the hope of renewal.

This, in fact, is the standard consistently invoked by Lefever and the norm by which his proposed reforms are to be measured. Lefever passes along the core theological perspective represented in this report:

> Men are often disillusioned by finding that changes of particular systems do not bring unqualified good, but fresh evils. New temptations to greed and power arise even in systems more just than those they have replaced because sin is ever present in the human heart. Many, therefore lapse into apathy, irresponsibility and despair. The Christian faith leaves no room for such despair, being based on the fact that the Kingdom of God is firmly established in Christ and will come by God's act despite all human failure.[41]

We are called to be obedient, not necessarily to be successful.[42] God will determine in his wisdom what and how he works through the secondary causes of his servants' activity. As Lefever, in a less pessimistic moment urges, "The millions of church members who are dissatisfied with WCC pronouncements should exercise all the democratic means at their disposal to see that the Council takes seriously the full range of views and experience represented among them."[43]

Notes

1. Ernest W. Lefever, *Nairobi to Vancouver: The World Council of Churches and the World, 1975–87* (Washington, D.C.: Ethics and Public Policy Center, 1987), 86.

2. *Constitution of the World Council of Churches* (as amended by the 9th Assembly, Porto Alegre, Brazil, February 2006), art. I. See also Martin VanElderen, *Introducing the World Council of Churches* (Geneva: World Council of Churches, 1990).

3. *Constitution of the World Council of Churches*, art. III.

4. *Constitution of the World Council of Churches*, art. V.1.a.

5. *Constitution of the World Council of Churches*, art. V.2.a.

6. *Rules of the World Council of Churches* (as amended by the 9th Assembly, Porto Alegre, Brazil, February 2006), art. V.1.

7. *Rules of the World Council of Churches*, art. XII.2,6.

8. *Rules of the World Council of Churches*, art. XIII.5.

9. *Rules of the World Council of Churches*, art. XIII.1.

10. *Rules of the World Council of Churches*, art. XIII.2.

11. World Council of Churches, *Report from the Public Issues Committee*, Ninth General Assembly, Porto Alegre, Brazil (February 23, 2006), Introduction, art. 2. Remaining references of particular sections of the PIC report will be made parenthetically by section and article number. See also J. A. Emerson Vermaat, *The World Council of Churches and Politics, 1975–1986* (Lanham: Freedom House, 1989).

12. Lefever, *Nairobi to Vancouver*, 56.

13. Walter Altmann, "Liberation Theology Is Alive and Well," *WCC Features* (November 16, 2009).

14. See the penetrating analysis in Gerard Berghoef and Lester DeKoster, *Liberation Theology: The Church's Future Shock* (Grand Rapids: Christian's Library Press, 1984). See also Vermaat, *The World Council of Churches and Politics*, 99: "Indeed, liberation theology is a manifestation of the transformation of the WCC from an ecclesiastical to a political organization."

15. Lefever, *Nairobi to Vancouver*, 81.

16. Lefever, *Nairobi to Vancouver*, 81.

17. See Ernest W. Lefever, *Amsterdam to Nairobi: The World Council of Churches and the Third World* (Washington, D.C.: Ethics and Public Policy Center, 1987), 1–3.

18. See above, chap. 3, "Relevance and Popularization."

19. Lefever, *Nairobi to Vancouver*, 58.

20. Lefever, *Nairobi to Vancouver*, 59.

21. Here the WCC invokes the authority of ecumenical patriarch Bartholomew that "water can never be regarded or treated as private property or become the means and end of individual interest" (5.5).

22. Victor V. Claar and Robin J. Klay, *Economics in Christian Perspective: Theory, Policy and Life Choices* (Downers Grove: InterVarsity Press, IVP Academic, 2007), 34.

23. Claar and Klay, *Economics in Christian Perspective*, 34.

24. Frank Rijsberman, "Sanitation and Access to Clear Water," in *Global Crises, Global Solutions*, ed. Bjørn Lomborg (New York: Cambridge University Press, 2004), 503.

25. "Expert Panel Ranking," in *Global Crises, Global Solutions*, 607.

26. John R. Schneider, "Christian Theology and the Human Ontology of Market Capitalism," *Journal of Markets & Morality* 10, no. 2 (Fall 2007): 279–98.

27. Schneider, "Christian Theology and the Human Ontology of Market Capitalism," 286.

28. Schneider, "Christian Theology and the Human Ontology of Market Capitalism," 291.

29. Schneider, "Christian Theology and the Human Ontology of Market Capitalism," 291.

30. Schneider, "Christian Theology and the Human Ontology of Market Capitalism," 295.

31. Lefever, *Amsterdam to Nairobi*, 55–61.

32. Lefever, *Nairobi to Vancouver*, 86.

33. Lefever, *Nairobi to Vancouver*, 84.

34. Lefever, *Nairobi to Vancouver*, 86.

35. On this see, for instance, Peter Kenny, "UN and WCC Heads Seek to Work Closer on Climate Change," *Ecumenical News International* (March 3, 2008), in which the UN Secretary General praises the "high moral power" of the WCC and the ability of the group to help further the UN's work.

36. Lefever, *Nairobi to Vancouver*, 85.

37. Lefever, *Nairobi to Vancouver*, 89.

38. Quoted in Lefever, *Amsterdam to Nairobi*, xi.

39. Lefever, *Nairobi to Vancouver*, 89.

40. See John Stott, *Christian Mission in the Modern World* (Downers Grove: InterVarsity Press, 1976). Cf. *The Laussane Covenant*, arts. 4, 5, 6, 7, 10, and 13.

41. *The Church and the Disorder of Society*, a report from the Amsterdam Assembly of the World Council of Churches, August 22–September 4, 1948. Quoted in Lefever, *Nairobi to Vancouver*, 7. Consider too the Old Testament motif of disobedience and periodic reform in the behavior of the people and the monarchy.

42. In another context, see also Richard A. Wynia, "Your Ecumenical Task," in *Seeking Our Brothers in the Light: A Plea for Reformed Ecumenicity*, ed. Theodore Plantinga (Caledonia: Inheritance Publications, 1992), 132: "the Lord does not ask for *success* in our work for Him; He asks for *faithfulness*."

43. Lefever, *Nairobi to Vancouver*, 11.

5

CONCLUSION:
AVENUES FOR REFORM

Who listens to the moral teachings
of Protestant churches?[1]

—James M. Gustafson

The preceding introduction, explication, and analysis of authoritative statements from the Lutheran World Federation, World Communion of Reformed Churches and its predecessors, and the World Council of Churches illustrates an underlying and basic agreement between institutions of the ecumenical movement on questions of social ethics and economics. We have found the whole-cloth economic narrative of the neo-Marxist ideology to be spread over the entire ecumenical movement. Likewise, rejection of neoliberal globalization has become the litmus test, the shibboleth, to determine authentic Christian belief.

The development of this feature of the ecumenical witness over the last fifty years attests to the ongoing influence of liberation theology on the movement. In line with the critique traced from Bonhoeffer, to Ramsey, to Lefever, we have shown this influence to have had seriously detrimental consequences, not least of which is the ongoing impotence, despite significant labor and toil to the contrary, of the ecumenical social witness. As Lefever observes, "the ecumenical movement's social witness has become obsolescent, marginal, irrelevant, or worse."[2]

It is in the hopes of correcting this defect in the work of the ecumenical movement that this critical engagement has been offered. It is by necessity a sketch of both the problems and potential solutions facing the ecumenical movement in the twenty-first century, but it is our fervent hope and prayer that updating and applying the critiques of Bonhoffer, Ramsey, and Lefever to the contemporary situation will have positive effects on the future development of the ecumenical movement's social witness. There are, indeed, any number of possible solutions to the various facets of the line of critique sketched in this engagement. At each level of the critique, from Bonhoeffer, to Ramsey, to Lefever, there is the real potential for correction of the defects in the ecumenical movement's social witness.

First, at the ecclesiastical level, where Bonhoeffer's question is at issue, the ecumenical movement might simply abandon claims to being an institutional form of the church. The ecumenical movement's embrace of its role as an apologist and popularizer of governmental and scientific expertise already pushes it in this direction. In this case, as Bonhoeffer notes, the ecumenical action "might have only a neutral character, not involving any confession, and this conversation might only have the informative character of a discussion, without including a judgement or even a decision on this or that doctrine, or even church."[3] However, the bulk of the ecumenical movement's self-understanding and tradition militates against abandoning such claims to institutional ecclesiastical authority, of one kind or another.

Therefore, second, at the ethical level, where Ramsey's critique is aimed more specifically, the ecumenical movement might well embrace this distinction between the institutional role of the church as a social witness and the political advocacy and social work of its members as the church manifests organically in society. The ecumenical movement might well, therefore, decline to issue doctrinaire and casuistical proclamations about this or that particular policy. Instead, the ecumenical movement would understand its role in this sphere to provide broad guidance rather than particular judgments. By outlining the broad parameters of acceptable Christian ethical and even economic thinking, for instance, the ecumenical movement's social witness would fiercely protect "room for legitimate disagreement among Christians and among other people as well as in the public domain—which disagreement ought to be welcomed and not led one way toward specific conclusions."[4] This kind of reform of the ecumenical movement's social witness would place correspondingly less emphasis on direct political engagement and advice, as offered for instance to the United Nations, and correspondingly greater emphasis on providing moral guidance to the church. The character of ecumenical statements on social issues under this kind of solution would be far more restrained and chastened than we find today.

Barring these reforms, there is still the third possibility, specifically pursued by Lefever's critique, for the ecumenical movement to correct its understanding of economic globalization and abandon the ideological neo-Marxist narrative. It would be no less wrong to make adherence to a neoliberal ideological view a matter of confessional integrity, but at least the major flaws of the revolutionary worldview of the ecumenical social witness could be, to one extent or another, mitigated. As Lefever writes, "Taking sides and not taking sides both have moral and political pitfalls. But supporting the wrong side is the worst of all options."[5] A richer dialogue and a constructive program of engagement with market economic theory might be undertaken by the ecumenical movement if it would leave off its attempts to turn the neo-Marxist narrative into a confessional absolute. In this sense, writes Lefever, "ecumenical leaders should make fuller use of the research and analysis of social, political, and economic issues generated by universities and public-policy research centers."[6] The point here is not to subsume the sovereignty and authority of the ecumenical social witness to economic or political experts of whatever ideological persuasion.

Rather, as Ramsey puts it, "the aim of these procedures and deliberations should not be to improve the church's speaking to the world its supposedly expert scientific advice, but to make sure that in everything addressed to the churches and to the world today our church councils can better speak *for* the church, for the whole of Christian truth, and every saving word but no more than can be said upon this basis."[7] In this way, writes Lefever, "the rich body of Christian social teaching needs to be studied, refined, and updated" in light of the findings of modern social and natural sciences.[8] The scientific findings themselves, however, do not determine the proper course of ethical decision-making. Therefore, Lefever concurs with Ramsey, that

> the primary obligation of the WCC in the political realm is to speak *to* its member churches, not *for* them. Council and denominational leaders should seek to clarify political and social issues in light of the Christian ethic and to motivate individuals to be responsible citizens. This is by far the most important task. WCC pronouncements should be more like papal encyclicals, which instruct the faithful in basic moral precepts and relate those precepts to current realities.[9]

It is in establishing those current realities that the findings of modern science play an important role, but in and of themselves these findings do not determine the content of Christian ethical thought.[10] This has all too often been the case, however, in the ecumenical movement's embrace of the basically economistic neo-Marxist worldview. In this regard, Lefever is right to point to Roman Catholic social teaching's valuation of the concept of prudence as instructive for the Protestant social witness.[11]

Without pursuing correctives along these general lines, the answer to Gustafson's challenging question, "Who listens to the moral teachings of Protestant churches?" will continue to be indeterminate, and deservedly so.[12] Without doing the hard work of serious ethical deliberation that engages a variety of conflicting perspectives, the ecumenical movement has little claim to possess authentic moral authority in the public square or among the churches. The specific suggestions that follow are intended to highlight some of the ways in which reform at each of these levels (ecclesiastical, ethical, and economic) might profitably be undertaken by the ecumenical movement in service to the entire church.

Service and Subsidiarity

As has been assumed throughout this critical engagement, the potential for the ecumenical movement to provide an important function in the life of the Protestant churches must be recognized. It is because there is so much promise in the ecumenical movement that reforms become so necessary.

A basic point of ecclesiastical correction that would improve the social witness of the ecumenical movement would be to chasten and humble the claims of the movement, not only in their particularity but in general. A dominant paradigm of the ecclesiological reality of the various ecumenical institutions is that of *communion*. The WCRC, for instance, identifies itself explicitly as "a communion of churches," as does the LWF.[13] As bodies united around a common confession, this identification makes sense. But confession is not the only biblical basis for communion. Indeed, the institution of the Lord's Supper as recorded in John 13 illustrates the inherent connection between *service* and communion. Knowing what was to befall him, the text relates that Jesus "got up from the meal, took off his outer clothing, and wrapped a towel around his waist. After that, he poured water into a basin and began to wash his disciples' feet, drying them with the towel that was wrapped around him" (John 13:4–5 NIV). John's account of the events at the Last Supper illustrate how intimately linked service and communion are to be for Christians, especially because Jesus enjoins us to continue to imitate him in both activities (Luke 22:19; John 13:15).

In this way, the key question for the ecumenical movement is how it can be of service to the member churches. One obvious answer is that it ought to take up tasks on behalf of the churches that they cannot do for themselves. Indeed, the ecumenical movement ought to limit itself to these kinds of activities. Otherwise, it tyrannizes the sovereignty of the member churches themselves. What this amounts to is a call for the ecumenical movement to embody the principle of *subsidiarity*.[14] This is a social, political, and ecclesiastical principle that finds its classic modern expression in Catholic social teaching, in which it takes the following formulation: "A community of a higher order should not interfere in the internal life of a community of a lower order, depriving the latter of its functions, but rather should support it in case of need and help to coordinate its activity with the activities of the rest of society, always with a view to the common good."[15]

Lesser known, however, is that the more remote origins of the principle of subsidiarity are found in the ecclesiastical and political thought of the Reformation. The development of Reformed political thought, particularly with regard to the concepts of federalism and subsidiarity, are often identified with the Dutch thinker Johannes Althusius.[16] The Renaissance and Reformation attempts to synthesize various sources from the history of legal and religious thought find expression to Althusius' *Dicaeologicae*, which itself "was an immense work (792 Latin folio pages) that sought to construct a single comprehensive juridical system by collating the Decalogue, Jewish law, Roman law, and various streams of European customary law."[17] In both theology as well as law, the topical method of organization, along with attention to the various streams of traditional precedents, set the stage for massive synthetic works such as Althusius' *Dicaeologicae*.[18]

Besides the pervasive influence of a scholastic method modified by the insights provided by Renaissance humanism, an important ecclesiastical source for the development of the concept of subsidiarity is embedded in a resolution passed in 1571 by the Dutch synod of Emden.[19] As Stephen J. Grabill puts it, this resolution was intended "to govern the relationship between parishes and general synods."[20] The first article produced by the Synod of Emden in 1571, for instance, has a textual predecessor in the *Wezelse Artikelen* of 1568.[21] Furthermore, we can trace the origins of the expression of subsidiarity present in the Emden resolution through the influence of earlier texts, themselves influenced by the Reformed churches in France.[22] Today, the WCRC Constitution itself contains clear testimony to this legacy in its statement, "no individual or church may claim or exercise dominance over another."[23]

In practice, the implementation of the principle of subsidiarity in the work of the ecumenical movement would mean that the primary task of the ecumenical bodies would be to take up legislative and deliberative questions that cannot be handled at the denominational or the congregational level. Ecumenical organizations should only seek to do things that member churches cannot do for themselves. A classic instance of this has to do with the question of ecumenical creeds and Protestant confessions of faith.

In 1998, the Interchurch Relations Committee (IRC) of the Christian Reformed Church in North America (CRCNA) received a letter from an Australian Reformed denomination (now called the Christian Reformed Churches of Australia, CRCA) asking for advice on a requested revision of the Apostles' Creed. In accord with their agreed on relationship, which includes the provision for "communication on issues of joint concern," the CRCNA approved the commission of a report by the IRC to investigate the matter.[24] The CRCNA report ultimately advised against the amendment of the Apostles' Creed by the CRCA. In part, this advice was based on the recognition that ecumenical creeds and Reformed confessions are not under the stewardship of any one denomination or church body. This is especially true in the case of an ecumenical creed such as the Apostles' Creed. Thus, the report judges that "the ecumenical creeds help to hold together a badly fragmented Christian church. Because the Apostles' Creed has ecumenical status in the Western church, the alteration of the 'descent' clause by one or more denominations would in effect place them creedally outside the circle of the worldwide church."[25] If the decision to amend confessional or creedal symbols is appropriate anywhere, it is at the ecclesiastical level that corresponds most closely to the extent that symbol is affirmed throughout the global church.

That is, an individual congregation or denomination cannot amend or modify a confessional symbol that it shares with other congregations or denominations without endangering the communion based on common confession. The wisdom of this recommendation shows sensitivity to the principle of subsidiarity and has implications for the handling of confessional questions by individual denominations in particular and the ecumenical movement in general. Discussions about the modification of common confessional symbols are best handled not only at the denominational or synodical level but also at the broader ecumenical level. At the very least, ecumenical organizations have a critical advisory or deliberative role to play in these kinds of discussions.[26] The lesson from this example is that unilateral action by individual denominations or congregations endangers confessional unity. Similarly, unilateral action or proclamation by ecumenical organizations and officials without the support of the member churches also undermines unity.

Law and Dignity

At the level of ethical deliberation, the theological doctrine of natural law has been receiving renewed attention in recent years, especially in Reformed theological circles.[27] As Gustafson has observed, if the characteristic of Roman Catholic moral thought is static stability, the characteristic of Protestant moral thought is dynamic flexibility. This is due in part, as Gustafson notes, to the modern Protestant "consensus on the rejection of the natural law tradition and particularly on the metaphysics of that tradition."[28] Corresponding to the responsibility to be informed about the latest developments in social and natural sciences is the responsibility to do the same with regard to theological dialogue. The contemporary Protestant endeavors to rediscover and reappropriate the natural-law legacy of the Reformation is just such a phenomenon that bears close attention by the ecumenical movement.[29]

One classical version of natural-law thinking took the form of the *ius gentium*, the so-called law of the nations. The idea was essentially that the common moral faculties shared by all human beings would, in general, create a broadly shared set of moral judgments. Jesus himself employs this kind of reasoning when he asks, for instance, that "if you greet only your brothers, what are you doing more than others? Do not even pagans do that?" (Matt. 5:47). In this case, Jesus employs pagan morality as a kind of argument from lesser-to-greater. The clear implication is that the morality of the Christian community is held to a higher standard.

113

In the same way, the ecumenical movement can be the forum in which to deliberate about the lower standard of the *ius gentium* in the world, making sure that the church, at least, is not worse than the pagans. The movement might also work to discern the *ius ecclesiasticum*, the law of the church. To be sure, agreement with the common consensus of the Christian church is not in and of itself a guarantee of correct moral conclusions, but as Lefever writes, "church councils would have much to gain by bringing in, or at least taking into account, laymen from all walks of life and all political persuasions."[30] This is one way to pursue the true *catholicity* of ecumenical moral deliberation, that which has been believed everywhere, always, by everyone (the Vincentian canon).

One of the positive results of an increased ecumenical engagement with the classic natural-law traditions is that it might well enhance the movement's efforts in the realm of human rights and human dignity.[31] Indeed, one of the workshops at the World Alliance of Reformed Churches 1977 General Council in St. Andrews, Scotland, recognized this possibility. The workshop on "Theology and Human Rights" specifically notes the value of such engagement, that "the discussion with other theological traditions such as the tradition of 'natural law,' of the 'two Kingdoms,' and so forth, would broaden and deepen our theological approach."[32] Once it has been understood that these traditions are not truly "other," as in belonging to the Roman Catholic or Lutheran traditions, but are instead also traditional Reformed approaches, the potential for fruitful engagement is greatly enhanced. As Ramsey writes, "Christians should be speaking more about order as a terminal political value along with justice, without the naïve assumption that these are bound to go together without weight given to both."[33] A vigorous engagement with the rich magisterial Protestant natural-law traditions would do a great deal to address such shortcomings.[34]

Wealth and Work

In the realm of economics, one must ask how the ecumenical movement can serve the church and in its public statements what it has uniquely to offer the world. On the latter question, it is in its relativization of economics that the ecumenical movement has the most to offer. This kind of proper valuation of penultimate concerns is only possible, of course, where they are understood to be such.[35] In this, correction of the ecumenical movement's basically economistic absolutization of neo-Marxist ideology is most necessary. It is precisely because love of God is to be foremost (Matt. 22:37) rather than love of money (1 Tim. 6:10) or some such other created thing that Christianity levels off and relativizes all other human realities. Bonhoeffer writes, "The ultimate and the penultimate are closely bound to one another. From this perspective the task is to strengthen the penultimate through a stronger proclamation of the ultimate and to protect the ultimate by preserving the penultimate."[36]

We are not, therefore, to simply equate the material wage earned, for instance, with the value of the work performed or the person performing the work. In a powerful statement of this perspective, Gerard Berghoef and Lester DeKoster write of work, the forms of which are "countless," as a "maturing of the soul," that

> liberates the believer from undue concern over the monotony of the assembly line, the threat of technology, or the reduction of the worker to but an easily replaceable cog in the industrial machine. One's job may be done by another. But each doer is himself unique, and what carries over beyond life and time is not the work but the worker. What doing the job does for each of us is not repeated in anyone else. What the exercise of will, of tenacity, of courage, of foresight, of triumph over temptations to get by, does for you is uniquely your own.

115

> One worker may replace another on the assembly line,
> but what each worker carries away from meeting the
> challenge of doing the day's shift will ever be his own.
> The lasting and creative consequence of daily work
> happens to the worker. God so arranges work that it
> develops the soul.[37]

But this kind of perspective is only possible within the context of a world-and-life view that affirms an anthropology consisting of both material and spiritual realities, of both body and soul.

In this way, the biblical perspective on wealth and work can be a powerful way to serve the church and its members, and through them the world at large. In order for the ecumenical movement to have a positive role to play in this respect, it must be able to properly account for the moral possibility that exists within the market economy. The complementary movements that are developing in the church known as "business as mission" and the "theology of work" are promising in this respect and, as such, deserve closer attention from the deliberative bodies of the ecumenical movement.[38]

Work and wealth must be understood not primarily as curses or marks of sinfulness but rather as blessings of God by which he sustains his material creation.[39] Bonhoeffer calls work, the secondary means through which God ordinarily provides our daily bread, an "order of grace."[40] This concept of work immediately brings to mind the concept of responsibility, of duty. Berghoef and DeKoster place the concept of work within the broader concept of stewardship, noting that "the basic form of stewardship is daily work."[41] This kind of balanced perspective on the grace God offers us through daily work and the realization of profit manifests the basic correctives that the ecumenical movement must embrace in order to live up to its own responsibility as an institution of global moral authority.

As Ramsey writes, this kind of responsible exercise of stewardship is critical to avoiding the pitfalls of hypocrisy. The ecumenical movement has "been calling for decades for responsible society, responsible government. It is high time for this judgment to be turned on ourselves. We should be resolved to say no more about responsibility in society until we have done something about responsible deliberation, and the procedures necessary for this to be made possible, at conferences sponsored by the churches, the NCC and the WCC."[42] Responsible deliberation must include a variety of viewpoints, including those that appreciate the merits as well as the dangers of the market economy.

The seventeenth-century theologian Richard Baxter sums up this vibrant theological perspective on wealth, work, and stewardship in his powerful sermon, "How to Do Good to Many" (1682).[43] On the proper relationship between temporal and eternal goods, the penultimate and the ultimate, Baxter advises, "Do as much good as you are able to men's bodies, in order to the greater good of souls. If nature be not supported, men are not capable of other good." He continues, "We pray for our daily bread before pardon and spiritual blessings, not as if we were better, but that nature is supposed before grace, and we cannot be Christians if we be not men; God hath so placed the soul in the body, that good or evil shall make its entrance by the bodily sense to the soul."[44] Moreover, Baxter places this relationship of ultimate to penultimate within the context of God's providential care. God condescends to use human beings as his agents for good work in the world. Baxter writes, "It is God's great mercy to mankind, that he will use us all in doing good to one another; and it is a great part of his wise government of the world, that in societies men should be tied to it by the sense of every particular man's necessity; and it is a great honour to those that he maketh his almoners, or servants, to convey his gifts to others." This kind of a perspective necessarily results in a generous spirit:

"God bids you give nothing but what is his, and no otherwise your own but as his stewards. It is his bounty, and your service or stewardship, which is to be exercised."[45] In this way, a perspective that takes into account the realm of work and the creation of wealth as a realm expressing God's grace is equipped to fruitfully and purposefully engage in the rigorous task of ethical deliberation.

The purpose of wealth in human life terminates on the aspect of stewardship consisting in generosity, and we can give only when we have resources out of which to give. The Old Testament tithe, for instance, has often been viewed as a minimum biblical standard for Christians to give as a reflection that, as Baxter puts it (drawing on Augustine before him), we give nothing back to God but what is his in the first place. The apostle Paul addresses the fundamental motive for giving in his second letter to the Corinthians: "Each man should give what he has decided in his heart to give, not reluctantly or under compulsion, for God loves a cheerful giver" (9:7 NIV). The theologian Ron Sider points out how unfaithful American Christians have been on this score. He observes that "if American Christians simply gave a tithe rather than the current one-quarter of a tithe, there would be enough private Christian dollars to provide basic health care and education to all the poor of the earth. And we would still have an extra $60 to 70 billion left over for evangelism around the world."[46] It is not only North America that has proven unfaithful in this regard. As Ram Gidoomal of the Lausanne Resource Mobilization Working Group writes, "Our poor understanding of the biblical command to give is reflected by the fact that from the $18.2 trillion earned annually by 2.2 billion Christians across the world, the current level of global giving to the church is less than 2.5% of income—well below the basic tithing levels." He goes on to observe that global church spending on missions ($23 billion) is surpassed by that spent on ecclesiastical crime ($25 billion).[47] Rather than focusing on advocacy toward various governmental bodies, the ecumenical movement would be better served to focus on the significant potential economic power of the church itself.[48] The ecumenical movement's message to the churches must be one that emphasizes giving as a response to God's overwhelming generosity to us in the gift of his Son.

Summary

The line of critique represented by Bonhoeffer, Ramsey, and Lefever engages the ecumenical movement at three different levels: the ecclesiastical, ethical, and economic. Correctives and reforms in answer to this engagement can be pursued at any and all of the three levels. Even so, there is an inner coherence to the critique, such that a comprehensive and thoroughgoing answer to this critical engagement should address all three sets of issues. One challenge that lies behind the entire line of critique is the ongoing influence of liberation theology on the ecumenical movement but more particularly in the expression of this influence in the instinct to turn economic opinions into matters of confessional integrity. The simplest and most effective way to move beyond the "fruitless combat" (Ramsey) of competing worldviews, the ideological conflict between neo-Marxism and neoliberalism, is to leave off the attempts to turn matters of moral prudence into matters in which the gospel is confessed to be at stake. Economic and political opinions should not be turned into articles of faith. Indeed, there must be room for bad economic and political opinions in our confession.[49] There are limits, of course, and these primarily arise when some alien influence or idea, a worldly ideology, takes the place of biblical confession and becomes an all-encompassing world-and-life view, a would-be competitor with Christianity.[50]

If a primary biblical image of disorder, confusion, and impiety is the human arrogance displayed at the Tower of

Babel, the key New Testament picture of renewed life together in Christ appears at Pentecost and the divine inspiration of Christian testimony. It is the fervent hope expressed in this critique that the divisive and ideological language of economistic faith, all too often expressed in the social witness of the ecumenical movement, might be renewed and reformed. Let our confession be not "I follow Marx," or, "I follow Hayek," "I follow Rand," or, "I follow Keynes," but rather, together, "We follow Christ" (see 1 Cor. 1:12). Ultimately our hope for unity lies not in ourselves or in any feeble human efforts, but in the power and providence of God, "who makes both us and you stand firm in Christ" (2 Cor. 1:26 NIV).

Notes

1. James M. Gustafson, *Protestant and Roman Catholic Ethics: Prospects for Rapprochement* (Chicago: University of Chicago Press, 1980), 130.

2. Ernest W. Lefever, *Nairobi to Vancouver: The World Council of Churches and the World, 1975–87* (Washington, D.C.: Ethics and Public Policy Center, 1987), 89.

3. Dietrich Bonhoeffer, "The Confessing Church and the Ecumenical Movement," in *No Rusty Swords: Letters, Lectures and Notes 1928–1936*, trans. Edwin H. Robertson and John Bowden, ed. Edwin H. Robertson (New York: Harper & Row, 1965), 331–32.

4. Paul Ramsey, *Who Speaks for the Church? A Critique of the 1966 Geneva Conference on Church and Society* (Nashville: Abingdon Press, 1967), 19.

5. Ernest W. Lefever, *Amsterdam to Nairobi: The World Council of Churches and the Third World* (Washington, D.C.: Ethics and Public Policy Center, 1979), 54.

6. Lefever, *Amsterdam to Nairobi*, 56.

7. Ramsey, *Who Speaks for the Church?* 43.

8. Lefever, *Amsterdam to Nairobi*, 56.

9. Lefever, *Amsterdam to Nairobi*, 58.

10. It is at this point that Ramsey's critique of the use of experts to improve ecumenical proclamation is aimed.

11. See Pontifical Council for Justice and Peace, *Compendium of the Social Doctrine of the Church* (Washington, D.C.: USCCB Publishing, 2005), nos. 547–48. See also Samuel J. Gregg, "A Lost Opportunity: The *Compendium of the Social Doctrine of the Church*—A Review Essay," *Journal of Markets & Morality* 9, no. 2 (Fall 2006): 261–76. On the direct relationship between the ecumenical movement and the Roman Catholic Church on such issues, see Thomas Sieger Derr, *Barriers to Ecumenism: The Holy See and the World Council of Churches on Social Questions* (Maryknoll: Orbis, 1983).

12. Gustafson, *Protestant and Roman Catholic Ethics*, 130.

13. *World Communion of Reformed Churches (WCRC) Constitution* (proposed July 2009), art. III; and *Constitution of the Lutheran World Federation*, art. III.

14. On the civil and social implications of subsidarity, see Pierpaolo Donati, "What Does 'Subsidiarity' Mean? The Relational Perspective," *Journal of Markets & Morality* 12, no. 2 (Fall 2009): 211–43.

15. John Paul II, Encyclical Letter *Centesimus Annus* (May 15, 1991), no. 48. See also Piux XI, Encyclical Letter *Quadragesimo Anno* (May 15, 1931), no. 79: "Just as it is gravely wrong to take from individuals what they can accomplish by their own initiative and industry and give it to the community, so also it is an injustice and at the same time a grave evil and disturbance of right order to assign to a greater and higher association what lesser and subordinate organizations can do. For every social activity ought of its very nature to furnish help to the members of the body social, and never destroy and absorb them."

16. On Althusius see Stephen J. Grabill, "Introduction to Selections from the *Dicaeologicae*," *Journal of Markets & Morality* 9,

no. 2 (Fall 2006): 403–28; Thomas O. Hueglin, *Early Modern Concepts for a Late Modern World: Althusius on Community and Federalism* (Waterloo: Wilfrid Laurier University Press, 1999); Robert M. Kingdon, "Althusius' Use of Calvinist Sources in His *Politica*," *Rechtstheorie* 16 (1997): 19–28; and Charles S. McCoy, "The Centrality of Covenant in the Political Philosophy of Johannes Althusius," in *Politische Theorie des Johannes Althusius*, ed. Karl-Wilhelm Dahm, Werner Krawietz, and Dieter Wyduckel (Berlin: Duncker and Humblot, 1988), 187–99. See also Johannes Althusius, "Selections from the *Dicaeologicae*," trans. Jeffrey J. Veenstra, *Journal of Markets & Morality* 9, no. 2 (Fall 2006): 429–83; idem, *Politica methodice digesta of Johannes Althusius (Althaus)* (New York: Arno Press, 1979); idem, *Dicaeologicae libri tres* (Herborn, 1617); idem, *Politica methodice digesta* (Herborn, 1614).

17. Grabill, "Introduction to Selections from the *Dicaeologicae*," 406.

18. See Grabill, "Introduction to Selections from the *Dicaeologicae*," 406; and Harold J. Berman and Charles J. Reid Jr., "Roman Law in Europe and the *Jus Commune*: A Historical Overview with Emphasis on the New Legal Science of the Sixteenth Century," *Syracuse Journal of International Law and Commerce* 20 (Spring 1994): 1–31.

19. See Hueglin, *Early Modern Concepts for a Late Modern World*, 152.

20. Grabill, "Introduction to Selections from the *Dicaeologicae*," 412.

21. The text of concern reads, "Gheen Kercke sal over een ander Kercke, gheen Dienaer des Woorts, gheen Ouderlinck, noch Diaken sal d'een over d'ander heerschappie voeren, maar een yeghelijck sal hen voor alle suspicien, ende aenlockinge om te heeschappen wachten." See *Acta Emden 1571*, in *Kerkelijk Handboekje: bevattende de bepalingen der Nederlandsche synoden en andere stukken van beteekenis voor de regering der kerken*, ed. P. Biesterveld and H. H. Kuyper (Kampen: J. H. Bos, 1905),

art. 1; and *Wezelse Artikelen 1568*, in *Kerkelijk Handboekje*, art. 4.7,9; 5.19; 8.14,20. See also Joh. Jansen, *Korte verklaring van de kerkenordening* (Kampen: Kok, 1923), 358–60.

22. See Glenn S. Sunshine, *Reforming French Protestantism: The Development of Huguenot Ecclesiastical Institutions, 1557–1572* (Kirksville, Mo.: Truman State University Press, 2003), 11: "Specifically, this study highlights some important ways in which the *Eglises Réformées* introduced their own elements into Reformed ecclesiastical structures, notably by establishing the first system of synodical government in which no pastor or church was permitted to have de facto or de jure authority over another (that is, the first example of presbyterial polity) in church history. This in turn set a precedent for most other national Reformed churches in Western Europe." See also Sunshine (p. 29) on the Gallican Confession (1559) and its articulation of "the most fundamental principle of French Reformed polity: the absolute prohibition of hierarchy among churches and ministers (art. 30)."

23. *World Communion of Reformed Churches (WCRC) Constitution*, art. IV.B. Compare "The French Confession of Faith, 1559," in *Reformed Confessions of the Sixteenth Century*, ed. Arthur C. Cochrane (Louisville: Westminster John Knox, 2003) art. XXX, 155: "We believe that all true pastors, wherever they may be, have the same authority and equal power under one head, one only sovereign and universal bishop, Jesus Christ; and that consequently no Church shall claim any authority or dominion over any other."

24. *Acts of Synod 1999* (Grand Rapids: Christian Reformed Church, 1999), 576–77.

25. *Agenda for Synod 2000* (Grand Rapids: Christian Reformed Church, 2000), 227.

26. Contemporary examples in the Reformed world include debate over the status of the Belhar Confession as well as amendment of Heidelberg Catechism Q&A 80.

27. See Stephen J. Grabill, *Rediscovering the Natural Law in Reformed Theological Ethics* (Grand Rapids: Eerdmans, 2006); J. Daryl Charles, *Retrieving the Natural Law: A Return to Moral First Things* (Grand Rapids: Eerdmans, 2008); and David Van-Drunen, *Natural Law and the Two Kingdoms: A Study in the Development of Reformed Social Thought* (Grand Rapids: Eerdmans, 2010).

28. Gustafson, *Protestant and Roman Catholic Ethics*, 62.

29. On the magisterial Protestant reception of natural law, see John T. McNeill, "Natural Law in the Teaching of the Reformers," *Journal of Religion* 26, no. 3 (July 1946): 168–82.

30. Lefever, *Amsterdam to Nairobi*, 57.

31. The work of International Justice Mission, which focuses on advocacy within the rule of law understood as an expression of the objective and transcendent moral order, is instructive here. See Gary A. Haugen, *Just Courage: God's Great Expedition for the Restless Christian* (Downers Grove: InterVarsity Press).

32. "Theology and Human Rights," Workshop of the World Alliance of Reformed Churches General Council, St. Andrews, 1977. On the two kingdoms, see William J. Wright, *Martin Luther's Understanding of God's Two Kingdoms: A response to the Challenge of Skepticism* (Grand Rapids: Baker Academic, 2010).

33. Ramsey, *Who Speaks for the Church?* 156.

34. See here especially VanDrunen, *Natural Law and the Two Kingdoms*, 1–20. See also Herman Bavinck, *Essays on Religion, Science, and Society*, trans. Harry Boonstra and Gerrit Sheeres, ed. John Bolt (Grand Rapids: Baker Academic, 2008), 269–71.

35. See Bonhoeffer's essay, "Ultimate and Penultimate Things," in *Ethics*, trans. Reinhard Krauss, Charles C. West, Doulgas W. Scott, ed. Clifford J. Green, Dietrich Bonhoeffer Works 6 (Minneapolis: Fortress Press, 2005), 146–70.

36. Bonhoeffer, *Ethics*, 169. See also David VanDrunen, "The Importance of the Penultimate: Reformed Social Thought and

the Contemporary Critiques of the Liberal Society," *Journal of Markets & Morality* 9, no. 2 (Fall 2006): 219–49.

37. Gerard Berghoef and Lester DeKoster, *God's Yardstick* (Grand Rapids: Christian's Library Press, 1980), 19. See also Dietrich Bonhoeffer, *Life Together and Prayerbook of the Bible*, trans. Daniel W. Bloesch and James H. Burtness, ed. Geffrey B. Kelly, vol. 5, *Dietrich Bonhoeffer Works* (Minneapolis: Fortress Press, 1996), 76: "Even routine mechanical work will be performed more patiently when it comes from the knowledge of God and God's command."

38. See C. Neal Johnson, *Business as Mission: A Comprehensive Guide to Theory and Practice* (Downers Grove: InterVarsity Press, IVP Academic, 2010); David W. Miller, *God at Work: The History and Promise of the Faith at Work Movement* (New York: Oxford University Press, 2007); Darrel Cosden, *A Theology of Work: Work and the New Creation* (Eugene: Wipf & Stock/Paternoster, 2004); Kenneth A. Eldred, *On Kingdom Business: Transforming Missions through Entrepreneurial Strategies* (Wheaton: Crossway, 2003); Gene Edward Veith Jr., *God at Work: Your Christian Vocation in All of Life* (Wheaton: Crossway, 2002); and Miroslav Volf, *Work in the Spirit: Toward a Theology of Work* (Oxford: Oxford University Press, 1991).

39. See Brian Griffiths, *The Creation of Wealth: A Christian's Case for Capitalism* (Downers Grove: InterVarsity Press, 1984).

40. Bonhoeffer, *Life Together*, 77. This is an important point that bears consideration, for instance, at the 2010 Lutheran World Federation Assembly in Stuttgart, Germany, "Give Us Today Our Daily Bread." Contrast Jan Milič Lochman, "The 'Holy Materialism': The Question of Bread in Christian and Marxist Perspectives," in *Christian Ethics in Ecumenical Context: Theology, Culture, and Politics in Dialogue*, ed. Shin Chiba, George R. Hunsberger, and Lester Edwin J. Ruiz (Grand Rapids: Eerdmans, 1995), 320–29.

41. Berghoef and DeKoster, *God's Yardstick*, 17. For a valuable resource compiled with ecumenical sensibility, see *The NIV Stewardship Study Bible* (Grand Rapids: Zondervan, 2009).

See also Lester DeKoster, *Work: The Meaning of Your Life* (Grand Rapids: Christian's Library Press, 1982).

42. Ramsey, *Who Speaks for the Church?* 60–61.

43. Richard Baxter, "How to Do Good to Many, or, The Public Good Is the Christian's Life," in *The Practical Works of Richard Baxter*, ed. William Orme, vol. 17 (London: Duncan, 1830), 291–333.

44. Baxter, "How to Do Good to Many," 303.

45. Baxter, "How to Do Good to Many," 320.

46. Ron Sider, *The Scandal of the Evangelical Conscience: Why Are Christians Living Just Like the Rest of the World?* (Grand Rapids: Baker Books, 2005), 118–19.

47. Ram Gidoomal, "Sustaining Mission Work in the Light of Funding Challenges," forthcoming article in Christian Institute of Management publication. For more information about CIM, visit http://www.cimindia.in/.

48. This is more than simply a theological interest for the ecumenical movement. Just as mainline denominations in North America are facing declines in membership and contributions, the ecumenical movement faces similar challenges. See Stephen Brown, "WCC Told of 'Serious Concern' about Drop in Contributions," *Ecumenical News International* (September 15, 2009).

49. This mirrors Bonhoeffer's understanding of confession. See Eberhard Bethge, *Dietrich Bonhoeffer: A Biography*, rev. ed., trans. Eric Mosbacher et al. (Minneapolis: Fortress Press, 2000), 445: "Bonhoeffer maintained that the church must leave room for bad theologies, and that the better ones must not be allowed to expel the worse."

50. See the Accra Confession's "rejection" of and implied judgment of moral equivalence between "global neoliberal capitalism" and "absolute planned economies" (art. 19).

REFERENCES

Ecclesiastical Documents

Acta Emden 1571. In *Kerkelijk Handboekje: bevattende de bepalingen der Nederlandsche synoden en andere stukken van beteekenis voor de regering der kerken.* Edited by P. Biesterveld and H. H. Kuyper. Kampen: J. H. Bos, 1905.

Christian Reformed Church in North America. *Church Order and Rules for Synodical Procedure 2009.* Grand Rapids: Christian Reformed Church, 2009.

———. *Agenda for Synod 2000.* Grand Rapids: Christian Reformed Church, 2000.

———. *Acts of Synod 1999.* Grand Rapids: Christian Reformed Church, 1999.

"The French Confession of Faith, 1559." In *Reformed Confessions of the Sixteenth Century.* Edited by Arthur C. Cochrane. Louisville: Westminster John Knox, 2003, 141–58.

John Paul II. Encyclical Letter *Centesimus Annus* (May 15, 1991).

Lutheran World Federation. *Communion, Responsibility, Accountability: Responding as a Lutheran Communion to Neoliberal Globalization.* Edited by Karen L. Bloomquist. Geneva: Lutheran World Federation, 2004.

———. *Constitution of the Lutheran World Federation* (as adopted by the LWF Eighth Assembly, Curitiba, Brazil, 1990, including amendments adopted by the LWF Ninth Assembly, Hong Kong, 1997.

Piux XI. Encyclical Letter *Quadragesimo Anno* (May 15, 1931).

Pontifical Council for Justice and Peace. *Compendium of the Social Doctrine of the Church.* Washington, D.C.: USCCB Publishing, 2005.

Wezelse Artikelen 1568. In *Kerkelijk Handboekje: bevattende de bepalingen der Nederlandsche synoden en andere stukken van beteekenis voor de regering der kerken.* Edited by P. Biesterveld and H. H. Kuyper. Kampen: J. H. Bos, 1905.

World Alliance of Reformed Churches. *Power to Resist and Courage to Hope: Caribbean Churches Living Out the Accra Confession.* Edited by Patricia Sheerattan-Bisnauth. Geneva: World Alliance of Reformed Churches and Caribbean and North America Area Council, 2009.

———. "Message from the Global Dialogue on the Accra Confession." Johannesburg, South Africa, September 2009.

———. *The Accra Confession: Covenanting for Justice in the Economy and the Earth.* Accra: World Alliance of Reformed Churches, 2004.

———. "Theology and Human Rights." Workshop of the World Alliance of Reformed Churches General Council, St. Andrews, 1977.

World Communion of Reformed Churches. *World Communion of Reformed Churches (WCRC) Constitution* (proposed July 2009).

World Council of Churches. *The Church and the Disorder of Society.* First General Assembly, Amsterdam, The Netherlands, August 22–September 4, 1948.

———. *Report from the Public Issues Committee*, Ninth General Assembly, Porto Alegre, Brazil (February 23, 2006).

———. *Constitution of the World Council of Churches* (as amended by the 9th Assembly, Porto Alegre, Brazil, February 2006).

———. *Rules of the World Council of Churches* (as amended by the 9th Assembly, Porto Alegre, Brazil, February 2006).

World Council of Churches Central Committee. "Statement on Eco-Justice and Ecological Debt." Issued September 2, 2009.

Other Sources

Althusius, Johannes. "Selections from the *Dicaeologicae.*" Translated by Jeffrey J. Veenstra. *Journal of Markets & Morality* 9, no. 2 (Fall 2006): 429–83

———. *Politica methodice digesta of Johannes Althusius (Althaus).* New York: Arno Press, 1979.

———. *Dicaeologicae libri tres.* Herborn, 1617

———. *Politica methodice digesta.* Herborn, 1614.

Altmann, Walter. "Liberation Theology Is Alive and Well." *WCC Features* (November 16, 2009).

Aquinas, Thomas. *Summa Theologica.* New York: Benzinger Bros., 1948.

Baker, Hunter. *The End of Secularism.* Wheaton: Crossway, 2009.

Ballor, Jordan J. "The Aryan Clause, the Confessing Church, and the Ecumenical Movement: Barth and Bonhoeffer on Natural Theology, 1933–1935." *Scottish Journal of Theology* 59, no. 3 (August 2006): 263–80.

Baltzell, E. Digby. *Puritan Boston and Quaker Philadelphia: Two Protestant Ethics and the Spirit of Class Authority and Leadership*. New York: Free Press, 1979.

Baum, Gregory. *The Church for Others: Protestant Theology in Communist East Germany*. Grand Rapids: Eerdmans, 1996.

Bavinck, Herman. *Reformed Dogmatics*. Vol. 4, *Holy Spirit, Church, and New Creation*. Translated by John Vriend. Edited by John Bolt. Grand Rapids: Baker Academic, 2008.

———. *Essays on Religion, Science, & Society*. Translated by Harry Boonstra and Gerrit Sheeres. Edited by John Bolt. Grand Rapids: Baker Academic, 2008.

Baxter, Richard. *How to Do Good to Many, or, The Public Good is the Christian's Life*. In *The Practical Works of Richard Baxter*. Edited by William Orme. Vol. 17. London: Duncan, 1830, 291–333.

Berghoef, Gerard, and Lester DeKoster. *God's Yardstick*. Grand Rapids: Christian's Library Press, 1980.

———. *Liberation Theology: The Church's Future Shock*. Grand Rapids: Christian's Library Press, 1984.

Berkhof, Louis. *Systematic Theology*. Grand Rapids: Eerdmans, 1998.

Berman, Harold J., and Charles J. Reid Jr. "Roman Law in Europe and the *Jus Commune*: A Historical Overview with Emphasis on the New Legal Science of the Sixteenth Century." *Syracuse Journal of International Law and Commerce* 20 (Spring 1994): 1–31.

Bethge, Eberhard. *Dietrich Bonhoeffer: A Biography*. Revised edition. Translated by Eric Mosbacher et al. Minneapolis: Fortress Press, 2000.

Bhagwati, Jagdish N. *In Defense of Globalization*. New York: Oxford University Press, 2004.

Bhalla, Surjit S. *Imagine There's No Country: Poverty, Inequality, and Growth in an Era of Globalization*. Washington, D.C.: Institute for International Economics, 2002.

Bonhoeffer, Dietrich. *Act and Being: Transcendental Philosophy and Ontology in Systematic Theology*. Translated by H. Martin Rumscheidt. Edited by Wayne Whitson Floyd Jr. Dietrich Bonhoeffer Works 2. Minneapolis: Fortress Press, 1996.

―――. "The Confessing Church and the Ecumenical Movement." In *No Rusty Swords: Letters, Lectures and Notes 1928–1936*. Translated by Edwin H. Robertson and John Bowden. Edited by Edwin H. Robertson. New York: Harper & Row, 1965, 326–44.

―――. *Dietrich Bonhoeffer: Witness to Jesus Christ*. Edited by John W. de Gruchy. Minneapolis: Fortress Press, 1991.

―――. *Ethics*. Translated by Reinhard Krauss, Charles C. West, and Doulgas W. Scott. Edited by Clifford J. Green. Dietrich Bonhoeffer Works 6. Minneapolis: Fortress Press, 2005.

―――. *Life Together and Prayerbook of the Bible*. Translated by Daniel W. Bloesch and James H. Burtness. Edited by Geffrey B. Kelly. Dietrich Bonhoeffer Works 5. Minneapolis: Fortress Press, 1996.

―――. *No Rusty Swords: Letters, Lectures and Notes 1928–1936*. Translated by Edwin H. Robertson and John Bowden. Edited by Edwin H. Robertson. New York: Harper & Row, 1965, 326–44.

―――. *Sanctorum Communio: A Theological Study of the Sociology of the Church*. Translated by Reinhard Krauss and Nancy Lukens. Edited by Clifford J. Green. Dietrich Bonhoeffer Works 1. Minneapolis: Fortress Press, 1998.

―――. Ultimate and Penultimate Things." In *Ethics*. Translated by Reinhard Krauss, Charles C. West, and Doulgas W. Scott. Edited by Clifford J. Green. Dietrich Bonhoeffer Works 6. Minneapolis: Fortress Press, 2005.

Bradley, Anthony B. *Liberating Black Theology: The Bible and the Black Experience in America*. Wheaton: Crossway, 2010.

Brailsford, William M. "Ethics and Public Policy Center." In *American Conservatism: An Encyclopedia*, 284–85. Edited by Bruce

Frohnen, Jeremy Beer, and Jeffery O. Nelson. Wilmington: ISI Books, 2006.

Brown, Stephen. "WCC told of 'serious concern' about drop in contributions." *Ecumenical News International* (September 15, 2009).

———. "Global Protestant leader derides credit crunch 'rescue packages.'" *Ecumenical News International* (May 28, 2009).

———. "Faith leaders say G20 must deal with 'greed' of financial system." *Ecumenical News International* (March 30, 2009).

Carter, Craig A. *Rethinking Christ and Culture: A Post-Christendom Perspective*. Grand Rapids: Brazos Press, 2006.

Charles, J. Daryl. *Retrieving the Natural Law: A Return to Moral First Things*. Grand Rapids: Eerdmans, 2008.

Claar, Victor V., and Robin J. Klay. *Economics in Christian Perspective: Theory, Policy and Life Choices*. Downers Grove: InterVarsity Press, IVP Academic, 2007.

Conway, Martin. "Under Public Scrutiny." In *A History of the Ecumenical Movement, 1968–2000*. Vol. 3. Edited by John Briggs, Mercy Amba Oduyoye, and Georges Tsetsis. Geneva: World Council of Churches, 2004, 433–58.

Cosden, Darrel. *A Theology of Work: Work and the New Creation*. Eugene: Wipf & Stock/Paternoster, 2004.

DeKoster, Lester. *Work: The Meaning of Your Life*. Grand Rapids: Christian's Library Press, 1982.

———. *Communism and Christian Faith*. Grand Rapids: Eerdmans, 1962.

Dempsey, Michael T., Robin Klay, and John Lunn, "What Bearing, If Any, Does the Christian Doctrine of Providence Have Upon the Operation of the Market Economy?" *Journal of Markets & Morality* 8, no. 2 (Fall 2005): 481–519.

Derr, Thomas Sieger. *Barriers to Ecumenism: The Holy See and the World Council of Churches on Social Questions*. Maryknoll: Orbis, 1983.

Donati, Pierpaolo. "What Does 'Subsidiarity' Mean? The Relational Perspective." *Journal of Markets & Morality* 12, no. 2 (Fall 2009): 211–43.

Dulles, Avery. *Models of the Church*. Expanded edition. New York: Image, 2000.

Eldred, Kenneth A. *On Kingdom Business: Transforming Missions Through Entrepreneurial Strategies*. Wheaton: Crossway, 2003.

FitzGerald, Thomas E. *The Ecumenical Movement: An Introductory History*. Westport: Praeger, 2004.

Gidoomal, Ram. "Sustaining Mission Work in the Light of Funding Challenges." Forthcoming article in Christian Institute of Management publication.

Grabill, Stephen J. "Introduction to Selections from the *Dicaeologicae*." *Journal of Markets & Morality* 9, no. 2 (Fall 2006): 403–28.

———. *Rediscovering the Natural Law in Reformed Theological Ethics*. Grand Rapids: Eerdmans, 2006.

Green, Clifford J. *Bonhoeffer: A Theology of Sociality*. Grand Rapids: Eerdmans, 1999.

Gregg, Samuel J. "A Lost Opportunity: The *Compendium of the Social Doctrine of the Church*—A Review Essay." *Journal of Markets & Morality* 9, no. 2 (Fall 2006): 261–76.

———. *Economic Thinking for the Theologically Minded*. Lanham: University Press of America, 2001.

Griffiths, Brian. *The Creation of Wealth: A Christian's Case for Capitalism*. Downers Grove: InterVarsity Press, 1984.

de Gruchy, John W. *Confessions of a Christian Humanist*. Minneapolis: Fortress Press, 2006.

Gustafson, James M. *Protestant and Roman Catholic Ethics: Prospects for Rapprochement*. Chicago: University of Chicago Press, 1980.

Haugen, Gary A. *Just Courage: God's Great Expedition for the Restless Christian*. Downers Grove: InterVarsity Press.

Hayek, F. A. "The Intellectuals and Socialism." In *The Intellectuals: A Controversial Portrait*. Edited by George B. de Huszar. Glencoe: The Free Press, 1960, 371–84.

Hueglin, Thomas O. *Early Modern Concepts for a Late Modern World: Althusius on Community and Federalism*. Waterloo: Wilfrid Laurier University Press, 1999.

Jansen, Joh. *Korte verklaring van de kerkenordening*. Kampen: Kok, 1923.

Johnson, C. Neal. *Business as Mission: A Comprehensive Guide to Theory and Practice*. Downers Grove: InterVarsity Press, IVP Academic, 2010.

Johnson, James Turner. *Love and Society: Essays in the Ethics of Paul Ramsey*. Missoula: Scholars Press, 1975.

Kenny, Peter. "World Church Leader Urges Other Faiths to Join Christians on Climate." *Ecumenical News International* (February 23, 2010).

———. "UN and WCC Heads Seek to Work Closer on Climate Change." *Ecumenical News International* (March 3, 2008).

Kingdon, Robert M. "Althusius' Use of Calvinist Sources in His *Politica*." *Rechtstheorie* 16 (1997): 19–28.

Klay, Robin, and John Lunn. "The Relationship of God's Providence to Market Economies and Economic Theory." *Journal of Markets & Morality* 6, no. 2 (Fall 2003): 541–64.

Lefever, Ernest W. *Amsterdam to Nairobi: The World Council of Churches and the Third World*. Washington, D.C.: Ethics and Public Policy Center, 1979.

————. *Nairobi to Vancouver: The World Council of Churches and the World, 1975–87*. Washington, D.C.: Ethics and Public Policy Center, 1987.

Lessl, Thomas M. "The Priestly Voice." *Quarterly Journal of Speech* 75 (May 1989): 183–97.

Lochman, Jan Milič. "The 'Holy Materialism': The Question of Bread in Christian and Marxist Perspectives." In *Christian Ethics in Ecumenical Context: Theology, Culture, and Politics in Dialogue*. Edited by Shin Chiba, George R. Hunsberger, and Lester Edwin J. Ruiz. Grand Rapids: Eerdmans, 1995, 320–29.

Lomborg, Bjørn, ed. *Global Crises, Global Solutions*. New York: Cambridge University Press, 2004.

Lowe, Eugene Y. Jr. "From Social Gospel to Social Science at the University of Wisconsin." In *The Church's Public Role*. Edited by Dieter T. Hessel. Grand Rapids: Eerdmans, 1993, 226–44.

Machen, J. Gresham. *Christianity and Liberalism*. Grand Rapids: Eerdmans, 1923.

Martin-Schramm, James B. *Population Perils and the Churches' Response*. Geneva: World Council of Churches, 1997.

Metaxas, Eric. *Bonhoeffer: Pastor, Martyr, Prophet, Spy*. Nashville: Thomas Nelson, 2010.

MacIntyre, Alasdair. *After Virtue*. 2nd ed. Notre Dame: University of Notre Dame Press, 2003.

McCoy, Charles S. "The Centrality of Covenant in the Political Philosophy of Johannes Althusius." In *Politische Theorie des Johannes Althusius*. Edited by Karl-Wilhelm Dahm, Werner Krawietz, and Dieter Wyduckel. Berlin: Duncker and Humblot, 1988, 187–99.

McNeill, John T. "Natural Law in the Teaching of the Reformers." *Journal of Religion* 26, no. 3 (July 1946): 168–82.

Miller, David W. God at Work: The History and Promise of the Faith at Work Movement. New York: Oxford University Press, 2007.

Mshana, Rogate R. "The Current Economic Crisis, Its Causes, Its Impact and Possible Alternatives," a lecture at the 33rd Assembly of the United Congregational Church of Southern Africa, August 24, 2009, Molepolole, Botswana. Geneva: World Council of Churches, 2009.

Mueller, John T. Christian Dogmatics. St. Louis: Concordia, 1934.

Nelson, E. Clifford. The Rise of World Lutheranism: An American Perspective. Philadelphia: Fortress Press, 1982.

Nelson, Robert H. The New Holy Wars: Economic Religion vs. Environmental Religion in Contemporary America. University Park: Pennsylvania State University Press, 2010.

Niebuhr, H. Richard. "The Kingdom of God and Eschatology in the Social Gospel and in Barthianism." In Theology, History, and Culture: Major Unpublished Writings. Edited by William Stacy Johnson. New Haven: Yale University Press, 1996, 117–23.

———. Christ and Culture. New York: Harper, 1951.

———. The Social Sources of Denominationalism. New York: Henry Holt and Co., 1929.

The NIV Stewardship Study Bible. Grand Rapids: Zondervan, 2009.

Norman, Edward. Christianity and the World Order. New York: Oxford University Press, 1979.

Oberman, Heiko A. "From Protest to Confession: The Confessio Augustana as a Critical Test of True Ecumenism." In The Reformation: Roots & Ramifications. Translated by Andrew Colin Gow. New York: T&T Clark, 2004, 149–66.

O'Boyle, Edward J. "Requiem for Homo Economicus." Journal of Markets & Morality 10, no. 2 (Fall 2007): 321–37.

O'Donovan, Oliver. "Obituary: Paul Ramsey (1913–1988)." Studies in Christian Ethics 1, no. 1 (1988): 82–90.

Opocensky, Milan. "Address of the General Secretary." World Alliance of Reformed Churches 23rd General Council. Debrecen: Hungary, 1997.

Pangritz, Andreas. "Who Is Jesus Christ, for Us, Today?" In *Cambridge Companion to Dietrich Bonhoeffer*. Edited by John W. de Gruchy. New York: Cambridge University Press, 134–53.

Paterson, Gillian. "Chapter Four: Brave New World." In "The CMC Story, 1968–1998." *Contact*, nos. 161/162 (June-July and August-September 1998).

du Plessis, Stan. "How Can You be a Christian and an Economist? The Meaning of the Accra Declaration for Today." *Stellenbosch Economic Working Papers* (February 2010): 1–14.

Pradervand, Marcel. *A Century of Service: A History of the World Alliance of Reformed Churches, 1875–1975*. Grand Rapids: Eerdmans, 1975.

Ramsey, Paul. *The Essential Paul Ramsey: A Collection*. Edited by William Werpehowski and Stephen D. Crocco. New Haven: Yale University Press, 1994.

———. *Who Speaks for the Church? A Critique of the 1966 Geneva Conference on Church and Society*. Nashville: Abingdon Press, 1967.

Rijsberman, Frank. "Sanitation and Access to Clear Water." In *Global Crises, Global Solutions*. Edited by Bjørn Lomborg (New York: Cambridge University Press, 2004), 498–527.

Schjørring, Jens Holger, Prasanna Kumari, and Norman A. Hjelm, eds. *From Federation to Communion: The History of the Lutheran World Federation*. Minneapolis: Fortress Press, 1997.

Schmidtz, David. *Elements of Justice*. New York: Cambridge University Press, 2006.

Schneider, John R. "Christian Theology and the Human Ontology of Market Capitalism." *Journal of Markets & Morality* 10, no. 2 (Fall 2007): 279–98.

————. *The Good of Affluence: Seeking God in a Culture of Wealth.* Grand Rapids: Eerdmans, 2002.

Sell, Alan P. F. *A Reformed, Evangelical, Catholic Theology: The Contribution of the World Alliance of Reformed Churches, 1875–1982.* Grand Rapids: Eerdmans, 1991.

Sherman, Lawrence W. "Two Protestant Ethics and the Spirit of the Reformation." In *Restorative Justice and Civil Society.* Edited by Heather Strang and John Braithwaite. New York: Cambridge University Press, 2001, 35–55.

Sider, Ron. *The Scandal of the Evangelical Conscience: Why Are Christians Living Just Like the Rest of the World?* Grand Rapids: Baker Books, 2005.

Social Watch. "The Social Impact of Globalization in the World," *Social Watch Report*, no. 6 (2002).

Stott, John. *Christian Mission in the Modern World.* Downers Grove: InterVarsity Press, 1976.

Sunshine, Glenn S. *Reforming French Protestantism: The Development of Huguenot Ecclesiastical Institutions, 1557–1572.* Kirksville, Mo.: Truman State University Press, 2003.

VanDrunen, David. *Natural Law and the Two Kingdoms: A Study in the Development of Reformed Social Thought.* Grand Rapids: Eerdmans, 2010.

————. "The Importance of the Penultimate: Reformed Social Thought and the Contemporary Critiques of the Liberal Society." *Journal of Markets & Morality* 9, no. 2 (Fall 2006): 219–49.

VanElderen, Martin. *Introducing the World Council of Churches.* Geneva: World Council of Churches, 1990.

Van Reken, Calvin P. "Christians in This World: Pilgrims or Settlers?" *Calvin Theological Journal* 43, no. 2 (November 2008): 234–56.

————. "The Church's Role in Social Justice." *Calvin Theological Journal* 34, no. 1 (April 1999): 198–202.

Veith, Gene Edward Jr. *God at Work: Your Christian Vocation in All of Life*. Wheaton: Crossway, 2002.

Vermaat, J. A. Emerson. *The World Council of Churches and Politics, 1975–1986*. Lanham: Freedom House, 1989.

Volf, Miroslav. *Work in the Spirit: Toward a Theology of Work*. Oxford: Oxford University Press, 1991.

Wright, William J. *Martin Luther's Understanding of God's Two Kingdoms: A Response to the Challenge of Skepticism*. Grand Rapids: Baker Academic, 2010.

Wynia, Richard A. "Your Ecumenical Task." In *Seeking Our Brothers in the Light: A Plea for Reformed Ecumenicity*. Edited by Theodore Plantinga. Caledonia: Inheritance Publications, 1992, 131–33.

Zwaanstra, Henry. *Catholicity and Secession: A Study of Ecumenicity in the Christian Reformed Church*. Grand Rapids: Eerdmans, 1991.

About the Authors

Jordan J. Ballor is a doctoral candidate in Reformation history at the University of Zurich and in moral and historical theology at Calvin Theological Seminary. Jordan serves as associate editor of the *Journal of Markets & Morality*, a peer-reviewed academic journal promoting intellectual exploration of the relationship between economics and morality from both social science and theological perspectives. He has authored articles in academic publications such as *The Journal of Religion*, *Scottish Journal of Theology*, and *Journal of Scholarly Publishing*, and has written popular pieces for newspapers including the *Detroit News*, *Orange County Register*, and *The Atlanta Journal-Constitution*. Jordan was profiled in the book, *The Relevant Nation: 50 Activists, Artists and Innovators Who Are Changing The World Through Faith* (Relevant, 2006) and is a founding editorial board member of the Post-Reformation Digital Library. His scholarly interests include Reformation studies, church-state relations, theological anthropology, social ethics, theology and economics, and research methodology. Jordan is a member of Brookside Christian Reformed Church and he resides with his wife and two children in Wyoming, Michigan. This is his first book.

STEPHEN J. GRABILL serves as Senior Research Scholar in Theology at the Acton Institute, a Grand Rapids, Michigan-based think tank that integrates Christian worldview with economics for leaders in the church, academy, and business sectors. He is executive editor of the *Journal of Markets & Morality*, as well as General Editor of the *NIV Stewardship Study Bible*, an Evangelical Christian Publishers Association (ECPA) award-contending resource, and a founding board member of Stewardship Council, the producer of the study Bible and a leader in the development and delivery of stewardship resources. Dr. Grabill graduated from Calvin Theological Seminary with a doctorate in systematic theology, after having spent more than a decade exploring the insights of the Reformed tradition on ethics, politics, and culture. He is author of *Rediscovering the Natural Law in Reformed Theological Ethics* (Eerdmans, 2006) and editor of *Sourcebook in Late-Scholastic Monetary Theory* (Lexington, 2007).

Christian's ![LIBRARY PRESS]

Founded in 1979 by Gerard Berghoef and Lester DeKoster, **CHRISTIAN'S LIBRARY PRESS** has been committed to publishing influential texts on church leadership, the vocation of work, and stewardship for more than thirty years. During that time Berghoef and DeKoster wrote significant works including *The Deacons Handbook*, *The Elders Handbook*, and *God's Yardstick*, which still are in demand today. After the passing of Lester DeKoster in 2009, the imprint is now administered by the Acton Institute for the Study of Religion & Liberty. For more information about Christian's Library Press, visit www.clpress.com.

ACTON INSTITUTE

With its commitment to pursue a society that is free and virtuous, the **ACTON INSTITUTE FOR THE STUDY OF RELIGION & LIBERTY** is a leading voice in the international environmental and social policy debate. With offices in Grand Rapids, Michigan, and Rome, Italy, as well as affiliates in four other nations around the world, the Acton Institute is uniquely positioned to comment on the sound economic and moral foundations necessary to sustain humane environmental and social policies. The Acton Institute is a nonprofit, ecumenical think tank working internationally to "promote a free and virtuous society characterized by individual liberty and sustained by religious principles." For more on the Acton Institute, please visit www.acton.org.